Management Extra

MANAGING MARKETS AND CUSTOMERS

ELSEVIER

eLEARN

Pergamon
Flexible
Learning

AMSTERDAM • BOSTON • HEIDELBERG • LONDON • NEW YORK • OXFORD • PARIS •
SAN DIEGO • SAN FRANCISCO • SINGAPORE • SYDNEY • TOKYO

Pergamon Flexible Learning is an imprint of Elsevier
Linacre House, Jordan Hill, Oxford OX2 8DP, UK
30 Corporate Drive, Suite 400, Burlington, MA 01803, USA

First published 2006
Revised edition 2009

Notice
No responsibility is assumed by the publisher for any injury and/or damage
to persons or property as a matter of products liability, negligence or
otherwise, or from any use or operation of any methods, products,
instructions or ideas contained in the material herein.

British Library Cataloguing in Publication Data
A catalogue record for this book is available from the British Library

Library of Congress Cataloging-in-Publication Data
A catalog record for this book is available from the Library of Congress

ISBN: 978-0-08-055739-7

For information on all Elsevier Butterworth-Heinemann publications
visit our website at www.elsevierdirect.com

Printed and bound in Hungary

Management Extra

MANAGING MARKETS
AND CUSTOMERS

Contents

Activities

Figures

Tables

Series preface

Whether you are a tutor/trainer or studying management development to further your career, Management Extra provides an exciting and flexible resource helping you to achieve your goals. The series is completely new and up-to-date, and has been written to harmonise with the 2004 national occupational standards in management and leadership. It has also been mapped to management qualifications, including the Institute of Leadership & Management's middle and senior management qualifications at Levels 5 and 7 respectively on the revised national framework.

For learners, coping with all the pressures of today's world, Management Extra offers you the flexibility to study at your own pace to fit around your professional and other commitments. Suddenly, you don't need a PC or to attend classes at a specific time – choose when and where to study to suit yourself! And, you will always have the complete workbook as a quick reference just when you need it.

For tutors/trainers, Management Extra provides an invaluable guide to what needs to be covered, and in what depth. It also allows learners who miss occasional sessions to 'catch up' by dipping into the series.

This series provides unrivalled support for all those involved in management development at middle and senior levels.

Reviews of Management Extra

I have utilised the Management Extra series for a number of Institute of Leadership and Management (ILM) Diploma in Management programmes. The series provides course tutors with the flexibility to run programmes in a variety of formats, from fully facilitated, using a choice of the titles as supporting information, to a tutorial based programme, where the complete series is provided for home study. These options also give course participants the flexibility to study in a manner which suits their personal circumstances. The content is interesting, thought provoking and up-to-date, and, as such, I would highly recommend the use of this series to suit a variety of individual and business needs.

Martin Davies BSc(Hons) MEd CEngMIMechE MCIPD FITOL FInstLM
Senior Lecturer, University of Wolverhampton Business School

At last, the complete set of books that make it all so clear and easy to follow for tutor and student. A must for all those taking middle/senior management training seriously.

Michael Crothers, ILM National Manager

A customer facing culture

More and more managers are looking for customer focus to help fight the pressures of rising costs, global competition and falling sales. But it's not simply a case of trying to get closer to your customers. There are more strategic decisions that if made can make your marketing more lean, more focused and more successful.

This book explores what market orientation means and the key things you need to be able to do as a manager to make a difference.

Drucker neatly summarises a long-standing debate on the nature of markets, product development and the importance of the customer.

> **The aim of marketing is to know and understand the customer so well the product or service fits him and sells itself.**
> **Source:**
> **Peter F. Drucker**

As long ago as 1776 Adam Smith in *An Inquiry into the Nature and Causes of The Wealth of Nations* wrote about the requirement for companies to produce goods and services that their customers wanted and could pay for. This was a somewhat revolutionary approach in an era when customers were largely required to accept what they were given.

> 'Consumption is the sole end and purpose of all production and the interests of the producer ought to be attended to only so far as it may be necessary for promoting that of the consumer.'

Source: Adam Smith The Wealth of Nations, Book 4 Chapter VIII

Your objectives are to:

♦ understand market orientation and what it means for you

♦ recognise ways you can contribute to customer value in your organisation

♦ explore how to improve customer satisfaction and customer relationships

♦ evaluate your competitive advantage and changes that could be made to structure, products and services to enhance the offer

♦ identify techniques for developing new markets and products.

1 A framework for market orientation

What is market orientation?

Marketing can be viewed as:

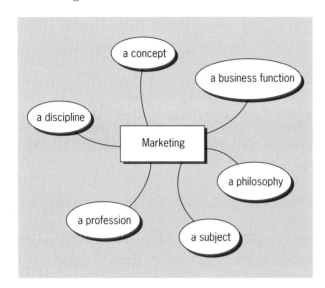

Figure 1.1 *The marketing concept*

This theme explores why marketing and customers are an important aspect of management and who your customers are. Without a clear understanding of the organisation's orientation towards its customers, a manager will fail to contribute effectively to its profitability and sustainability. This is presented as a framework for market orientation and is intended to support managers in making a contribution to the growth and development of the organisation.

The Chartered Institute of Marketing (CIM) definition below illustrates that marketing is much more than just a concept.

> Marketing is the management process responsible for identifying, anticipating and satisfying customer requirements profitably.

Source: Chartered Institute of Marketing (2006)

According to the CIM definition, marketing is actually a planned, organised and ongoing activity. If undertaken correctly, marketing can provide the organisation with the ability to differentiate and compete more effectively.

The strategic importance of pricing, branding and positioning is explored in this theme to set the context for profitability and growth.

In this theme you will:

♦ **Learn about market orientation and what it means for you as a manager**

♦ **Understand the marketing mix and its contribution to growth and development**

♦ **Recognise and develop customer groups and set aims, targets and conditions for success**

♦ **Understand what resources are required for effective market orientation.**

The shape of marketing

Organisations that have successfully adopted the marketing concept are said to be market oriented. This means they have progressed from focusing on what they can make and then trying to sell it, to supplying what they know customers actually want. There is a long history behind the study of market orientation. Some of the key milestones are:

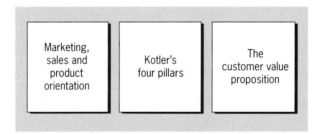

Figure 1.2 *Frameworks for marketing*

Marketing, sales and product orientation

Frameworks for marketing can be oriented in a number of ways, all of which at some point in the life cycle of an organisation can have a value.

Some organisations are said to be product-led which means that focus is given to making superior products.

Some organisations are sales-led, which suggests they place some emphasis on persuading customers to buy using a range of communication methods.

Marketing-led organisations develop their products or services to meet the needs of the customer.

All of these types of orientation have a place in the market economy, but product and sales orientation are likely to need to give way to marketing orientation at a point in the product lifecycle.

Product Orientation	Sales Orientation	Marketing Orientation
Product-led organisations focus on what they can make and on improving the product over time (perhaps this product-led approach is due to their expertise or resources, or maybe because this is how it has always been done in the company).	Sales-led organisations place the emphasis on aggressive selling and/or promotion (on the assumption that their sales efforts will help them to gain an advantage over the competition).	Marketing-led organisations focus on the needs of their target customers and aim to provide products and services that meet those needs at a profit (which usually involves planning and research).

Table 1.1 *Types of orientation*

The main difference between a marketing-led organisation and a sales or product-led organisation, is that the former has both the desire and the ability to understand and fulfil customer needs. Rather than trying to manufacture or sell something that does not meet the needs of the marketplace, marketing orientated organisations make an effort to understand the marketplace and the various external environmental changes that might present opportunities or that might pose threats in the future.

Key Point: The marketing concept involves matching the internal strengths and resources of an organisation, to the opportunities that exist in the external environment.

Organisations that embrace the marketing concept aim to identify the internal strengths of the organisation, so that they can be matched to the external opportunities that exist. At the same time, they aim to identify any internal weaknesses, so that they can be minimised in order to reduce the effect of any external threats.

In this way, an organisation can work to its strengths and take advantage of any assets and competencies it holds, provided of course these assets and competencies are considered attractive to the market.

The four pillars

For Kotler (1997), the marketing concept rests on 'four pillars': the target market, customer needs, integrated marketing and profitability.

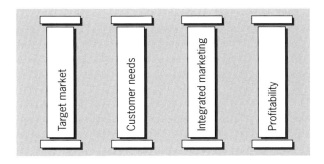

Figure 1.3 *Four pillars*

1. **Identify and define your target market** No organisation can operate successfully in every market because product or service is not for everybody. Organisations do best when they define their target markets and implement a tailored marketing program.

   Example from a publishing company:

   > A good example is a title about how to find a job. The author could say that everyone needs to get a job at some point, so the title is good for all adults. He or she might seek a heavy, broad promotional campaign selling the title's detailed information on writing resumes and cover letters and conducting interviews successfully.
   >
   > But the publisher knows that the broad market of job-seeking adults is divided into a variety of target segments. These could include adults, college students and blue-collar workers. Other niches that would be interested in buying career-oriented books include colleges, outplacement firms and state governments.

2. **Determine your customers' needs** A quick analysis points out segments with widely varying needs. So, the obvious next step is to determine what those needs are.

   Continuing with the publishing example let's first look at the college market, which has various buyers with diverse needs.

   - College teachers are looking for books that could be used as textbooks or for supplementary material. They need information that is presented sequentially, discussion questions at the end of each chapter and perhaps an accompanying instructor's guide.
   - Students need concise, clear and inexpensive information that will give them the facts they need to find a job quickly.
   - Career placement officers need to increase the number of college students that graduate with jobs.
   - Alumni associations need to provide alumni with useful information that will increase the value of their Alma Mater and increase the size of donations to the school.
   - College bookstores want to make a profit selling books.

   As you can see, buyers in any one segment have varying needs. Selling to all of them with the same literature and the same appeal will do little to increase your sales. Marketing to them, according to their individual needs, will have much better results. Understand the buyers in each of your target segments and market to them as individuals and you will sell more products or services.

3. **Integrated marketing** The organisation following a marketing concept would not end the strategy here. All parts of the marketing process must be coordinated or the results will be diluted. There are four parts that must be integrated into marketing campaigns: the product and its distribution, price and promotion. We will look at these in more detail later.

4. **Profitability** This is the end goal, but may not be the short-term goal. The aim is to set up processes and systems that will generate profits, but not at the expense of customer satisfaction and doing the right things.

These pillars remain the key tenets of a market and customer oriented approach, but they have been refined by organisations and theorists.

A new approach to the definition of marketing

After considering many definitions of marketing, McDonald & Wilson (2002) proposed a new marketing definition as follows:

Marketing is a process for:

♦ Defining markets – quantifying the needs of the customer groups (segments) within these markets.

♦ Determining the value propositions to meet these needs.

♦ Communicating these value propositions to all those people in the organisation responsible for delivering them and getting their buy-in to their role.

♦ Playing an appropriate part in delivering these value propositions to the chosen market segments.

♦ Monitoring the value actually delivered.

Referring specifically to the function of marketing, McDonald & Wilson (2002) also emphasise that:

'…it will be ineffective unless the whole company is market driven ('customer driven', 'customer-needs driven', 'demand driven' are other expressions for the same thing). This market-driven philosophy has to be led from the board downwards.'

Source: McDonald & Wilson (2002)

Defining markets and understanding value

This usually means focusing on a market or a segment of a market and making an effort to understand what value (such as the benefits from the product or service) the customers want or need. An important part of this process is also the identification of the critical success factors i.e. one or more of the key things an organisation must get absolutely right in order to compete successfully in a market or a market segment.

Determining the value propositions

Having understood what value or benefits the customer wants, an organisation needs to examine:

♦ how the industry structure might change (use of electronic delivery channels)

♦ the value to be delivered which could be related to the 4 C's i.e. 'Cost', Convenience', 'Communications' and 'Consumer wants and needs' as identified by Schultz, Tannenbaum & Lauterborn (1993).

The outcome is likely to be a strategic marketing plan covering the next 3 years.

Deliver value propositions

Based on the strategic plan, value can be delivered by considering the sequence of activities by which an organisation transforms its inputs into outputs of a greater value. Examples include:

♦ research and development

♦ inbound and outbound logistics (how goods and services are moved around)

♦ service levels

♦ the ingredients in the product or service mix

♦ the supply chain

♦ the use of technology to support operations.

Monitoring the value

Monitoring can take various forms and this particular stage emphasises the cyclical nature of the overall process.

It is important to monitor and assess the current view of the value required by customers and whether this has changed over time.

The organisation will also probably want to monitor the value it receives against the marketing objectives such as the volume of sales by product type, or the assessment of customer profitability.

Monitoring value may also involve the analysis of customer-based measures specific to the organisation, which may, for instance, be known as Customer Lifetime Values (CLV), Customer Relationship Management (CRM) or key account criteria.

This basic process of reviewing customer needs, planning, delivering and monitoring forms the framework for most marketing activities and focuses attention on the value that the organisation can provide to its customers.

Activity 1
The customer value proposition

Objectives

This activity will help you to:

◆ explore your own and your organisation's customer value proposition

◆ understand the importance of the customer and any other priority stakeholders.

Task

1 Why is the customer the most important person a company has to deal with? Write down some notes about the way your organisation perceives its customers.

2 What is the orientation of the organisation – product, sales or market/customer led?

3 The decision to buy

Put yourself in the purchasing position. Which of the following would contribute to your decision to buy a holiday or not from a particular company assuming location and price were about right?

☐ A tourism or travel association guarantee

☐ Good before-sales service

☐ The assurance of good after-sales service

☐ Additional facilities or activities offered as part of the purchase price

☐ Special transport arrangements

☐ A cash discount

☐ Vouchers or gifts on purchase

☐ Discounts on future holidays

☐ Good credit facilities

☐ Good reputation of the provider

☐ Persuasive advertising

☐ Ease and convenience of purchase

☐ Online payment security guarantees

☐ Pleasant surroundings

4 Think benefits not products

Outline the features and benefits for customers of your main products or services. The aim here is to identify the value proposition and the first stage is to think benefits.

Service or product	Features	Benefits
Example from a hotel room rental service	Family rooms available with interconnecting doors	Children safe and close by Parents' peace of mind

5 What services or goods are combined with the proposition offered by your company to add value. Think here about the four C's i.e. 'Cost', Convenience', 'Communications' and 'Consumer wants and needs' as identified by Schultz, Tannenbaum & Lauterborn (1993).

What service levels do you provide and are they the services that customers want?

Core service	Value added through			
	Cost	Convenience	Communications	Consumer wants and needs

Feedback

You have been asked to think carefully about your own and your organisation's attitudes to customers and the benefits you can provide to your customers. A definition of the value that your organisation's products or services can add is an important first stage of the market oriented framework.

The decision to buy – this example highlights the range of reasons with which an individual will come to the purchasing decision. Having made a basic decision about the price and location of the holiday there may be many reasons why you chose the one you did, or you chose not to take the holiday with a particular organisation. Similar forces are at work when individuals and organisations prepare to buy from you. The essence of a good marketing framework is to define the value proposition so that you know what your customers value most highly and you are in a position to make precisely that offer clearly and succinctly.

It may be worth checking the features and benefits you have identified with others in the organisation or even with customers. Are your perceptions the same as theirs?

The marketing mix

Developing and maintaining a balanced and appropriate marketing mix is crucial to marketing and business success.

To achieve marketing success, the right product must be presented to the right people in the appropriate manner, at the right price, at the right time. If a supplier can bring all of these different processes and elements together in a complementary manner, the resulting marketing mix could be a source of considerable competitive advantage.

What is the marketing mix?

Although the marketing mix can be the source of competitive advantage, the marketing mix can also be viewed as a management tool. Each individual element of the marketing mix should be analysed and if necessary, adapted to ensure that the right balance is achieved to give the product or service the very best chance of success in the market place.

The traditional marketing mix is also sometimes referred to as the 4 Ps as illustrated below.

Marketing mix element	Description and relevance of the Marketing Mix Element
PRODUCT	This relates to the nature or quality of the product or service concerned and/or the image that may be associated with users or consumers of the product or service. Besides understanding how a product or service can meet the basic needs of customers, marketers also need to consider the relative position held by their product or service in a given market, compared to alternative products or services that might be available from the competition.
PRICE	This relates to the market price of the product or service and pricing policy. Marketers need to ensure that their product or service is priced appropriately, so that both sales and also acceptable profits are achieved. Products or services may be priced at different ends of the price spectrum depending on the nature of the product or service offering, the perceived status of the supplier, or the pricing tactics and strategies adopted by competitors.
PLACE	This relates to the manner in which a given product or service is distributed to the consumer or the end user. For various reasons, some suppliers will distribute their products or services via a network of distributors, while others will supply their product or service direct to the consumer or end user. Decisions concerning the distribution of products or services will be taken in the light of various factors such as the nature of the product or service, the resources available to the organisation concerned, or because of opportunities presented by the availability of new technology.
PROMOTION	This relates to the manner in which the product or service is promoted to wholesalers, to retailers or to consumers/end users (which of course depends on the nature of the distribution policy and other factors). Since promotion is a term that is used to encompass advertising, personal selling, sales promotion, direct marketing, public relations and other methods of customer communication, this element of the marketing mix is also sometimes called the 'The Communications Mix'.

Table 1.2 *The traditional marketing mix (the 4 Ps)*

After considering the various elements of the traditional marketing mix, you may start to appreciate that each of the 4 elements are related to each of the other elements of the mix. In other words, if one element is changed in some way, it will have an effect on one or more of the other elements of the mix.

For instance, if after appropriate research has been conducted, it is decided that a product should be improved and re-positioned in the marketplace, in order to appeal to a slightly different market, consideration must also be given to the other elements of the marketing mix. Although the successful re-positioning of a product is not easy to achieve, some motor manufacturers such as Skoda and Seat have managed to gain some success in re-positioning their car ranges.

When re-positioning a product that involves an improvement in product quality together with the aim of enhancing market perception of the product, it is very likely that the price will need to be increased. The price increase will be needed to recover the additional costs involved in re-development and also to more closely match the prices offered by competitors. Under these circumstances, although customers would no doubt prefer lower prices, increased prices are also likely to match customer expectations i.e. customers will expect to pay more for improved quality and conversely may associate lower prices with lower quality.

Apart from adjusting the price in the light of a change to the product, the other elements of the marketing mix might also need some adjustment. Under the circumstances, the distribution policy might need to be more exclusive, perhaps involving the use of only a small number of carefully selected distributors for the improved product. The promotional mix might also need to be re-formulated, so that the content of the messages emphasises the features and benefits of the re-positioned product. Even the promotional methods and communications channels used to promote the product would probably need to be re-considered, so that they match the new product image.

A successsful mix

The increase in service sector businesses has led to the development of the extended marketing mix. This very briefly incorporates three new factors. People, processes and physical evidence.

Extended Element	Description and relevance of the Extended Marketing Mix Element
PEOPLE	This relates to the people employed within the organisation, to individuals associated with the organisation, or any other relevant personal stakeholders. Because people can add value through superior service and effective communication and because people are often the interface between customer and supplier, the importance of all employees should never be underestimated. Individuals should be clear about their own role and responsibilities and how they can add value for the benefit of everyone (perhaps by improving service levels, quality, making suggestions etc).
PROCESSES (or PROCESS)	This relates to any process connected to the marketing function i.e. any processes that might involve the customer and which could take place before, during or after a sale. It is often said that many great products or services have failed because efficient and effective processes or systems did not support these products. Processes and/or systems must make it easy for the customer to communicate, or easy for the customer to buy.
PHYSICAL EVIDENCE	This relates to the visual impression gained as a result of exposure to a range of physical evidence as diverse as vehicles, buildings, the decoration or cleanliness of offices, rooms or venues, the quality and style of stationery and written materials and the nature, style and cleanliness of clothing worn by representatives of a particular organisation. Just like all the other elements of the marketing mix, this element needs to be compatible with the others in the marketing mix or the organisation concerned.

Table 1.3 *The extended marketing mix*

The marketing mix is a useful analytical tool for managers and marketers alike. It forms the basis for many of the decisions made about an organisation's direction.

Activity 2
The marketing mix

Objectives

This activity will help you to understand how the marketing mix works in practice.

Task

1 In each of the following scenarios identify the elements of the marketing mix that are being analysed and resolved.

Scenario 1 – The marketing team were keen to define the product in less than ten words. They had discovered during market research that people found it difficult to say what the product was never mind what it could do for them.

Scenario 2 – Financial control measures were being put in place in the organisation. If spiraling costs weren't reduced the offer would have to be changed and that might mean going into whole new markets. It had been a tempting thought that a higher value product might be the next move, but research suggested that competitors in the higher level market were struggling even more than they were.

Scenario 3 – The issue wasn't about the service or even how it was delivered. There was a general malaise, triggered by a few key people leaving, and this was translating into fewer orders.

Scenario 4 – They just couldn't get enough goods to the shops. It might sound like an enviable position, but it actually meant lost sales. They needed a new system for ordering, perhaps including advance ordering and different distribution channels to supplement those that they were using.

2   What elements of the marketing mix are a priority for consideration in your organisation?

Feedback

1   In each of the scenarios there are specific issues that need to be addressed. These can be related to one or more of the areas of the extended marketing mix. Compare your answers to those that follow.

Scenario 1 – In this case the issues are product definition and promotion. The product is ill defined and the messages being communicated are confusing. Without clarity from the manufacturer the customer will be unclear about the product.

Scenario 2 – Product and price are in question here. The product definition is wavering if they are considering giving it a significantly higher value. Price reduction may be required to get the goods moving again.

Scenario 3 – This is about people in the organisation believing in the service being provided. The impact of a general malaise, especially among those interfacing with customers can be significant.

Scenario 4 – This is about place and processes. The distribution channels are not working and they are right not to just focus on the logistics of getting the products to the shops, but to think of new ways of getting the goods to the end users. This will involve new processes for ordering, returns and marketing.

2   Using the information from the marketing mix you should be able to identify at least one issue for your oganisation related to marketing your product or services. Think about whether any other factors come into play. It is rare that a single factor is causing a problem.

What managers need to know

Although a manager's specific role in market orientation will depend on their role and function within an organisation, there are good reasons for all managers to be keenly interested in this fundamental element of the business. Piercy (2002) offers a review of what he thinks managers need to know in the process of going to market.

Category	The Details
Customers	Understanding customers and focusing on the market offering we make to them and what it produces in superior customer value.
Market strategy	Choosing market targets and building a strong market position based on differentiating capabilities to create a robust and sustainable value proposition to customers driven by networks of critical relationships.
Implementation	Driving the things that matter through the corporate environment to the marketplace.

Table 1.4 *What managers need to know*   Source: Adapted from Piercy (2002)

Piercy believes that managers do not need to get involved in the technical detail, so in his opinion they do not need to know in detail about pricing theories, market research techniques, advertising theory, buyer behaviour models and so on.

Piercy takes a skeptical view of marketing theory, but the point is well made that customer focus is central to the organisation's survival and prosperity. Marketing cannot exist in a vacuum, separate from other functions. Marketing orientation is a culture that needs to be adopted at all levels and in all areas of the organisation to be effective. It is an overriding business philosophy that applies to internal customers (other functions within an organisation) as well as to external customers. It will also impact on the way an organisation works with its suppliers.

Internal and external customers

Customers come in all shapes and sizes and managers first need to recognise who their customers are. Internal customers matter and the relationships developed internally can mean the difference between implementation and collapse. An internal customer is anyone for whom you provide a service within the organisation. It is as important to understand their wants and needs as your external customers and thereby create a culture that supports delivery of the right products and services.

Overcoming barriers to successful market orientation

Few intend to put up barriers to the delivery of a good service, but practice and tradition can lead to the development of a number of barriers. It is arguably one of the key leadership roles of a manager to help break down these barriers.

Culture

Culture is intrinsically rooted in the organisation but may be working against a corporate view of customer value. Structural changes may be required to realign the organisation to focus employees on the customer. Mission, vision and objectives can be altered to draw attention to the requirement to meet customer needs. Capital investment projects need to clearly target improvements in customer service. Too often organisations will implement a new process for stock taking or customer ordering and in the process of development lose sight of the ultimate goal. Logistical efficiencies may be delivered at the cost of customer satisfaction.

When cultural differences emerge, the result may be power battles and political infighting. None of which are likely to support customer needs. A manager's insight and leadership is required to see beyond vested interests and refocus on objectives.

Decision-making

Managers need to make the decisions required to see through complex action plans and strategies. Marketing has developed techniques and tools that are very specialised and require specialist analysis. The role of the manager is not to undertake the analysis but to use the results to inform and develop strategies for implementation. Effective use of specialist support is essential to ensure that decisions are made, delays are reduced and action is taken. Knowing how much you need to know is one part of this process and knowing where to get the information is the other.

Resources and skills

Having the right resources, people, information systems in place to help make the decisions can also be a barrier for many cash strapped organisations. A manager needs to be in a position to negotiate for appropriate resources and information. It's a balancing act between a realistic assessment of the information and resources available and the potential value of additional or other resources to improve customer service.

The role of the manager is to facilitate, to get the best out of people and to recognise opportunities. The manager in any function will need to create an environment where directed and strategically focused action can take place and to identify areas in which the organisation will need specialist expertise in marketing or selling.

Resources may be required to find out more about the customer, to help individuals understand their customers or to find out more about what competitors are doing. This may include bringing in expertise such as market researchers, branding and pricing specialists.

Product decisions may involve legal advice to ensure compliance, patent and copyright issues are sorted out. Resources for promotions may include:

◆ advertising including e-advertising, TV and newspaper advertising

◆ direct marketing including telemarketing and e-marketing

◆ selling face to face

◆ maintaining effective public relations

◆ selling via brochures, exhibitions and events

◆ sponsoring events or related products

◆ packaging the product using text, images, colour and shape.

Today's customer is almost as concerned about how the offer is delivered, where it is sited, and the channel by which they order it, as price. Customers are busy, discerning and well-informed. Easy ordering and delivery with a high quality of service are often a deciding factor for them. Any framework for marketing orientation needs to consider carefully IT, packaging, distribution, logistics and merchandising.

Resources required to support people in the organisation include IT systems, Customer Relations Systems and training.

Activity 3
A manager's role

Objectives

This activity will help you to:

◆ define the limits and scope of your responsibility for marketing orientation and customer focus

◆ understand the contribution you can make to customer focus in your organisation.

Task

1   The aim of this activity is to outline your responsibilities and where you would bring in other resources and expertise to support growth and development in the organisation.

Who are your customers?

Internal customers

External customers

2   What elements of your role as a manager are directed towards customers?

3   What barriers do you need to overcome?

Cultural

Decision-making

3 What resources and skills do you think could contribute to the development of customer focus in your organisation?

Feedback

It may seem strange to think about these areas of the business if you do not have a direct responsibility for marketing in your organisation. The aim of this activity is to support you in recognising that you do have a role and you can make a contribution. There may be elements of the marketing mix that you can affect. You may but able to support a cultural change towards a customer focus. You may be able to spot a barrier to organisational goals that others cannot see.

Customer characteristics

An important principle in marketing is focus and in particular the need to focus on a specific group (or groups) of potential customers. Usually potential customers are categorised into groups, whose members have various common characteristics.

It is usually far more effective and efficient to identify and select a particular section of the market that will become the focus of marketing activities, than to expect to appeal to every single member of the population. This is because very few (if any) organisations can successfully meet the needs of everyone, in part because they simply do not have the resources to do so. So, marketing is about recognising that only a proportion of the population will ever be potential customers and that only a percentage of these will become customers of a particular business.

What is segmentation?

The market can be split into 'segments' by using a range of different segmentation criteria. In practice it is unlikely that one single segmentation variable will be used to categorise a group of potential customers, as one single segmentation variable such as age, will usually be far too general.

A number of segmentation variables usually need to be combined to develop the profile of a typical customer. In this way, the marketing effort can be designed to appeal to the target market segment.

The availability and use of new technologies and systems does enable some organisations to both identify and profile potential customers more easily than ever before. The challenge to marketers and managers however, is to constantly remain in touch with the technologies involved and the possible benefits and disadvantages each might bring.

The different types of customer

A market may consist of a group, or groups of customers that can be described as market segments. These customers can be 'segmented' by a various criteria and each different market segment may respond to communications, in a different manner. That means communications should be specifically designed and targeted and based on a sound understanding of the individuals, or the organisations involved.

Broadly speaking, markets fall into:

◆ 'Personal' Segments (often called 'Consumer' Segments)

◆ 'Business' Segments (often called 'Corporate' Segments)

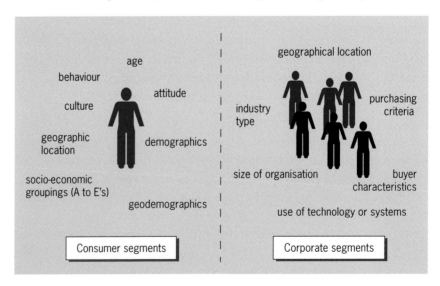

Figure 1.4 *Segmentation*

1 A framework for market orientation

Understanding consumer segments

A market can consist of a wide range of individuals each with different characteristics and preferences. A market segment on the other hand, consists of group of individuals that have common characteristics and is therefore a sub-group. The characteristics shared by the sub-group will not be shared by the market as a whole.

Consumers can be segmented (grouped) in many ways, including by:

◆ age

◆ attitude

◆ behaviour

◆ culture

◆ demographics

◆ geographic location

◆ geodemographics (e.g. ACORN and Pinpoint)

◆ socio-economic groupings (A to E's).

Understanding business segments

Corporate customers can also be grouped in many ways including by:

◆ buyer characteristics (either individual or DMU characteristics)

◆ geographical location

◆ industry type

◆ purchasing criteria (large or small purchase/quality standards etc)

◆ size of organisation (measured by staff levels, turnover, profits or outlets)

◆ use of technology or systems.

What is targeting?

Targeting follows the process of segmentation. Targeting is about focusing marketing effort and any marketing communications on the most profitable and potentially productive market segments.

How to target the most appropriate segments

There are some important factors to consider if targeting is to be precise and effective. These factors are:

◆ segment attractiveness and viability

◆ segment size and growth potential

◆ segment profitability

◆ segment identity and compatibility.

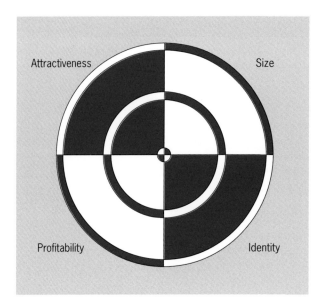

Figure 1.5 *Targeting*

Segment attractiveness and viability

Market segments will appear attractive if there are external opportunities that match the internal strengths of the organisation concerned. Low cost airlines operate efficiently on a low cost basis and the positioning of their service appeals to a market segment that appreciates the 'low cost, no frills approach'.

Besides this matching process, there also needs to be a sufficient number of people within the chosen market segment, to make the operation viable. The low overheads of the airlines' operations and their ability to communicate successfully with a selected nationwide audience, is a major factor in their success.

Segment size and growth potential

Research needs to be conducted to establish the size of the targeted market segment and its potential for growth. Unless there is significant potential, either for gaining an appropriate share of the market within the segment, or for growing the market segment, other options should be considered.

Segment profitability

When deciding to enter new markets, it is usual to prioritise by ranking key factors. A key factor when prioritising these potential foreign markets is the issue of market profitability.

Segment compatibility

This compatibility or 'degree of fit' between the chosen market segment and the supplier or a product or service, should be as close and meaningful as possible. Compatibility is a question of determining whether you have the right set of skills, resources and competencies to deliver the service or products.

Match makers

Depending on the resources of the organisation and the opportunities available, various targeting options can be evaluated. The following three issues should therefore also be considered when embarking on the targeting process:

♦ Matching resources with opportunities

♦ Targeting individual segments

♦ Targeting multiple segments

Matching resources with opportunities

Very few organisations have the resources or the desire, to target the whole market for a given product or service. Even if extensive resources do exist, because of the need to identify with the target market, some form of selective targeting will usually exist.

Targeting individual segments

There are many different bases for segmenting of the market, although one segmentation variable might be far more important than any other.

For example, one possible target market segment for a holiday tour operator promoting a 'summer sun vacation' might look something like this:

Age:	18 to 30
Gender:	Male
Socio-economic groups:	C2/D/E
Neighbourhood:	urban dwellers
Occupation:	manual/unskilled/students in higher education

Even though a number of segmentation variables are involved, they combine to form one single target market segment, which is then targeted by the tour operator.

Targeting multiple segments

Multiple segments may include presenting a clearly defined offer to a range of customers. Amazon for instance provides a range of categories based on age, subject, media, authors, and type of goods. The aim is to make as many customers as possible feel able to find the category of goods they are looking for whilst seeing the full range available to them from the website.

Activity 4
Knowing your customers

Objectives

This activity will help you to:

◆ understand more about your customers and how they are segmented and targeted

◆ explore how target setting contributes to the success of the organisation.

Task

Your task is to find out as much information as you can about a significant customer. You may find you need to ask someone in the marketing department, someone in sales or consider an internal customer that you know well.

1 Identify one of your organisation's main customers?

2 How are customer groups segmented and in what segment does this customer fall?

3 What are this customer's needs?

4 What benefits does the customer prioritise?

Customer	Customer segment	Customer needs	Benefits prioritized by the customer

5 Summarise the nature of your target segments, their viability, size, profitability, growth potential, compatibility and identity

6 Given all of this information note down at least three ways in which targeting contributes to the success of the organisation or three ways targeting could be used more effectively.

1

2

3

Feedback

Segmentation and targeting may look like a precise science, but customers are fickle and for ever chainging their wants and needs. Your role as a manager is try to keep up with the customers, by carrying out an analysis like this regularly. It is beneficial whether you work with internal or external customers. It will also help you to predict where they are going next. A very useful piece of analysis is to be looking at the benefits perceived by customers from your products and services. It may be worth finding out if there is any current market research on what your customers really think. For internal customers it may be of value to ask them.

Action list

Review the activities you have completed for this theme and write down any action points that you can use to support you and your team in creating or improving the market or customer focus in your organisation.

◆ Recap

This theme begins to establish a framework for marketing and customer focus in an organisation. The central tenet of the framework is that customer focus needs to be embedded throughout the organisation and not imposed from above, or implemented in a crisis.

Learn about market orientation and what it means for you as a manager

- Market orientation impacts on all levels and all the individuals in the organisation.

- The concept of customer focus should permeate all the objectives, attitudes and behaviours exhibited in the organisation.

- As a manager there are a number of roles you can take to contribute to customer focus, such as supporting new attitudes, overcoming barriers, working effectively with colleagues and internal customers and most of all understanding customers.

Understand the marketing mix and its contribution to growth and development

- The extended marketing mix encourages managers to think about a range of issues in the analysis and development of a product or service.

- The mix consists of product, price, place, promotion, people, processes, physical evidence.

Recognise and develop customer groups and set aims, targets and conditions for success

- Understanding your customers is a pre-requisite for market and customer orientation.

- The analysis of segments and strategies for targeting are useful tools for developing your customers and tracking their needs and wants. This will help you to set conditions for success.

Understand what resources are required for effective market orientation

- Resources to support an organisation fully develop and grow their customer bases are reviewed.

- Resources may be in the form of expertise such as market research and PR. They can also be in the form of information, budgets and people.

 **More @**

McDonald, M. and Wilson, H. (2002) *The New Marketing*, **Butterworth-Heinemann**
The New Marketing presents a comprehensively revised blueprint for the marketing process affected by technological developments and the associated 'information revolution'. Built around the leading concept of a value exchange with customers, it provides essential advice on how to harness the latest technology and incorporate it effectively into marketing practice.

Piercy, N. F. (2002) *Market-Led Strategic Change: A Guide to Transforming the Process of Going to Market*, **Butterworth-Heinemann, pp. 7–11**
This books takes a fresh approach to the concept of marketing and seeks to debunk some of the myths. It has a central focus on customer value and creative strategic thinking in the context of realistic and practical examples.

Porter, M. E. (1980) *Competitive Strategy: Techniques for Analysing Industries and Competitors*, **Free Press**
A seminal text on strategies to support growth and development. Its focus is on analysis of the business environment and how organisations perform.

Institute of Sales and Marketing Management www.ismm.co.uk [accessed January 2006]

Chartered Institute of Marketing (2002) www.cim.co.uk [accessed January 2006]

What's New In Marketing (WNIM) www.wnim.com [accessed January 2006]

Full references are provided at the end of the book.

2   Customer value

Creating a customer culture

Creating a customer culture is a hard won battle, but there are three basic resources in your armoury.

♦ Happy employees = better customer service

♦ Customer-based values

♦ Key account/customer relationship management

This theme evaluates how, as a manager, you can make an effective contribution to customer satisfaction in your organisation. It includes concepts such as valuing front line staff at all levels, creating a shared vision and understanding of how staff will work with customers, sharing values and beliefs with your customers, key account management and customer relationship management.

Interactions with customers can be at a range of levels and in a variety of relationships. To conclude the theme, we look at the emergence and potential of the partnership as a new way of working with both customers and suppliers to improve service.

In this theme you will:

♦ **Learn about the factors you can influence that make customers satisfied**

♦ **Evaluate your understanding of your own and your customers' values**

♦ **Understand the importance of key account and customer relationship management**

♦ **Assess relationships between customers and suppliers within partnerships.**

Happy employees

An organisation that is operating well will have fundamentally happy, motivated employees and an atmosphere of respect. Creating that organisational culture is a responsibility of the management team across all functions in the organisation. A culture characterised by support for both internal staff, suppliers and customers is likely to perform well in terms of satisfying customers.

The internal environment

Examining the internal organisational environment Kotler and Andreasen (1995) outline the factors that contribute to a customer focus with both satisfied employees and satisfied customers.

Figure 2.1 *The internal environment for customer focus*

Top management support

A company will not become customer focused until its leaders believe in it, understand it and want it. The mind-set and the tone of the organisation needs to be set from the top and permeated through its managers and employees. The tone is likely to be a positive one where people have respect for one another and value what each other does.

Effective organisation design

A well-structured company will contribute to this tone and the focus on customers. There is no one perfect design and it may not include a marketing department, but it does need to include people in senior positions who make a point of knowing and finding out what the customer needs and the changing customer perspectives. In many organisations departments are organised to respond to the needs of particular segments of their market.

In-company marketing training

Organisational awareness of marketing and market orientation can contribute to increased understanding of the importance of customer focus. Training in market awareness will help all employees to see where the organisation fits in the wider market and how they are contributing to the process. Messages that reinforce the concept and reward customer focused behaviours will support this process in the longer term.

A recent analysis of over 6,000 companies, by the PA Consulting Group showed that marketing, broadly defined, typically drives three times more value than cost efficiency. If this is the case do we value marketing and customer focus highly enough? And if not we ought to make more noise about it.

Better employee hiring practices

Kotler and Andreasen also propose a review of hiring practices. Instead of replacing new employees on a like for like basis every organisation needs to consider the dynamics of the market place and whether alternative skills or new attitudes could contribute more to the culture and skills base. New employees also need to be hired on the basis of their customer focus and responsiveness to customer needs, as well as for skills that in some cases could be easily learned. An organisation that is able to meet its employee's needs is likely to be able to retain staff to build longer lasting relationships.

Rewarding market oriented employees

Creating effective reward strategies is always a difficult balancing act. Rewards can be perceived in a number of ways. They can be valued or devalued based on the way they are delivered. Monetary and motivating rewards may be successful but ultimately unsustainable. Rewards may be capable of persuading people to emulate behaviours or set the bar too high leading to demotivation. Well planned, consistently applied and rewards valued by employers and employees alike do however work. The important part of the message is not that an individual has gained an award, it is rather that they have gained an award for displaying a particular behaviour. In this case, a behaviour that benefits customers as well as the organisation and supports longer-term relationships with valued customers. A number of companies are moving towards rewards based on customer satisfaction ratings rather than, or as well as, financial targets.

Planning system improvement

Finally, a well functioning organisation does not rest on its laurels. Rather it focuses on the internal and external environment to spot changes, opportunities and threats. Kotler and Andreasen look to the organisation's planning system to strengthen the capture and interpretation of information about customers and the market. By involving everyone in the organisation in the process of using marketing information the company will gain a better picture of the improvements it can make.

Happy employees = better customer service

What's New in Marketing website looked at the nature of customer-facing businesses.

> Research by a number of organisations has revealed that if you want to have happy customers, particularly in a customer-facing business environment, then you should be doing your utmost to make sure that your employees feel happy too, that their opinions are valued and respected; so that they become integral to the company, and more loyal as a result. The benefits of employee involvement are wide-ranging, and this includes a significant reduction in absenteeism. It can also increase the productivity of your employees.

Source: www.wnim.com/archive

They also reviewed what it is about employee involvement and consultation that works well and why it sometimes doesn't work.

What works well and why?	Why does information and consultation fail?
Working together to build a shared view of the business and its competitive environment	A lack of commitment from senior managers
Sharing information widely to enable all participants to have a shared grasp of the context within which decisions are being made	A failure to consult at an early enough stage and before the key decisions are made
Consultative processes which enable the workforce both individually and as a whole to contribute effectively to the debate on issues and to influence the outcomes	No dynamism – keep going around the same issues
A range of joint problem solving techniques to address issues	Poor agenda
Feedback systems enabling employee voice to be heard effectively and get messages back to the workforce	Little or no training in information and consultation for participants (both managers and employee representatives)
	Too much pressure on time and resources for participants
	A failure to follow up on promises or actions
	A lack of supportive infrastructure

Table 2.1 *Employee involvement and consultation*

Source: 'High Performance Workplaces; Informing and Consulting Employees, The IPA's response to the DTI's consultation document' (2003)

Communication and consultation form the basis for a customer-focused approach. The levels and standards of service need to be agreed throughout the organisation to ensure that they are achievable, profitable and sustainable. They then need to be communicated throughout the organisation so that everyone knows their role in providing the service to clients and customers. This

31

strategy should signal to everyone the priority given to customer focus in the corporate plan.

An illustration of a customer focused approach appears here from The Times 100. The example is from Travis Perkins, a UK building and plumbing merchant.

A quality focus

Travis Perkins is organised in such a way as to give customer focus a priority. It is important therefore to develop performance indicators to measure the achievement of customer focus. Ongoing performance of the organisation and its component parts can then be measured in terms of achievement of these performance targets. Comparisons can be made between the performance of individual stores, and parts of these stores. Benchmarking can be employed to communicate best practice enabling ongoing organisational improvement.

Customer Service Groups provides a structure for serving customers. Performance Indicators are established for Customer Service Groups and regular meetings take place within the Groups to plan research, review the results of research, review actions to improve customer service and review performance, as well as planning ongoing improvements, and the establishment of priorities. The CSG's are thus a form of Quality Circle focused on making customer service processes more effective.

The Customer Service Groups are a form of democratic organisation, in which members interact by sharing ideas and working in a collaborative way to the benefit of the company.

Rather than using external market research organisations to find out information about customers and their requirements, Travis Perkins prefers to build relationships with customers at point of sale in a personal way. Building ongoing relationships to find out about customer issues enables individual stores and the organisation as a whole to build relationships based on listening to customers. This is all part of the customer-focused structure of the organisation.

Travis Perkins is successful because the emphasis in organising the organisation is on building the organisation around customer service. Satisfied customers are likely to purchase more, and to purchase regularly rather than using rival firms. The result is that turnover and profit increases, enabling the company to generate higher growth and pay higher dividends to shareholders.

Source: www.thetimes100.co.uk/teachers

Activity 5
A customer-focused approach

Objectives

This activity will help you to:

◆ identify ways in which you can influence attitudes amongst your team

◆ understand the importance of the internal relations in generating a customer-focused approach.

Task

1 Indicate on the list below what infrastructure you have in place to support customer focus.

☐ Top management support

☐ Effective organisation design

☐ In-company marketing training

☐ Better employee hiring practices

☐ Rewarding market-oriented employees

☐ Planning system improvement

2 To how many of the following questions can you categorically answer 'Yes'?

☐ Are your processes really customer driven? (Or are they driven by what is in the best interest of your organisation?)

☐ Does your service quality approach allow for flexibility and variability at the point of customer interaction?

☐ Does your data collection promote qualitative feedback about how the customer feels about your service?

☐ Is customer retention one of the key drivers in how you measure the effectiveness of your organisation?

3 Using the table below identify ways in which you can support your team and improve customer service – either to internal or external customers. Think about your current situation and use the example in Table 2.1 to help you.

What works well and why?	Why does information and consultation fail?

4 Outline any changes you could make to improve the commitment to a customer-focused approach.

Feedback

The aim of this activity is to provide structure to your analysis of your current situation. Your responses will be individual to you. Can you see ways in which barriers are being set up either against the people who need to provide a service or by organisational structures? You should be starting to think about the ways you can work with your team to contribute more effectively to the customer focus in your organisation.

Customer-based values

Here are two propositions to evaluate:

- ◆ Teams that share values are likely to work together better than those who do not.

- ◆ Organisations that share values with their customers and express those values are more likely to have a meaningful relationship.

Consider how far you agree with these statements.

The aim is to look at the values that we share amongst ourselves and the values that we share with our customers. Research findings suggest that to provide service quality managers need to create related, but different, climates: a climate for employee well being and a climate for service. Satisfied employees are motivated to deliver high service value, this in turn leads to satisfied customers, which in turn is more likely to lead to a wider public perception of the value of the organisation and its products or services.

Team values

People tend to get along and work well with people who are perceived to share common values and tend to conflict with, avoid, and reject those who are perceived to hold opposing values. Teams work well together when the 'espoused values' are reflected in the 'actual values' shown in the behavior of members. Organisations thrive and adapt to a changing environment when, for example, values associated with maintaining stability are balanced with values promoting creativity and change, values promoting group solidarity are balanced with values promoting individualism and risk, and values promoting prominence and power are balanced with values which support listening, caring, trust, and dedication.

Source: www.leader-values.com/Content

The journey begins with a clearly defined sense of purpose, supported from within at the highest levels. Customer focus and market orientation cannot be imposed.

There are a number of trigger points for a re-evaluation of the organisation and its employee's self image.

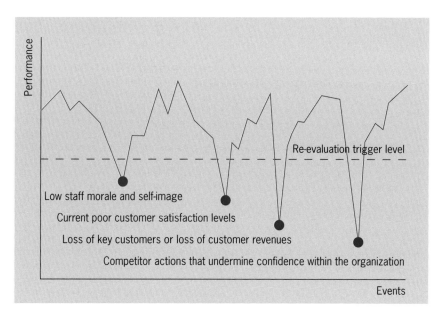

Re-evaluation trigger level

Low staff morale and self-image

Current poor customer satisfaction levels

Loss of key customers or loss of customer revenues

Competitor actions that undermine confidence within the organization

Events

Figure 2.2 *Trigger points for a re-evaluation*

It may be tempting to think that the fault lies with the product, the service, the price or the prevailing market conditions. It could be any or all of these things, but it could also be a fundamental lack of trust or belief in the product or service from employees. Organisations relate to customers in many ways and it would be unrealistic to think that any are perfect. What makes organisations that succeed stand out is the widely held belief that everyone is working towards a common and respected goal.

Addressing the needs and values of the internal teams dealing with customers is a first priority. There are three key messages that employees need to understand to help develop confidence and trust:

◆ That they and their work is valued and respected and they are contributing to goals that will benefit themselves and the organisation

◆ That they are empowered to take action to rectify customer dissatisfactions

That they will be listened to when they feedback or communicate.

What is more is each of these messages is within the sphere of influence of any manager in the organisation and is not restricted to the remit of the sales or marketing team.

Proctor (2000) outlines a number of strategies he defines as internal marketing that will contribute to employee satisfaction and empowerment.

◆ Informing the internal market about the organisation's mission and its role within it.

◆ Ensuring that internal information and communication channels work effectively in order to sell ideas and services internally.

- Implementing special motivation programmes directed at front line service providers that recognise that front line personnel form a critical means of meeting competition.

- Recognising a greater desire on the part of employees to play an active role in all aspect of work life that affects them.

- Auditing employer – employee interactions: training and communications.

- Using mass communication techniques e.g. newsletters, intranets, notice boards, about new marketing strategies, organisational policies and plans etc to provide employees with helpful information.

- Viewing the development of knowledge and skills in employees as an investment rather than a cost.

- Motivating employees through reward incentives to provide excellent service.

- Continually trying to define employees, management's perceptions and expectations of them.

- Establishing a network service that answers employees' questions, fields their complaints, remedies situations and alerts top-level management to potential trouble spots in employees' concerns.

- Seeking employee suggestions as to changes and improvements that would be beneficial in improving the level of customer service.

Sharing values with customers

Customers may value the relationship they have with their supplier because, for instance, they know that they are getting a good price. Alternatively, they may value the relationship principally because they know they are getting locally produced goods. In each of these cases, the employees in the supplier company need to know and also value the service they are able to offer. They need to know their customers and that this is the service the customer is particularly looking for.

On the basis of this information an employee will be able to quickly tell whether the customer shares the values they can offer and if not what other offers they can make. The pivotal points are that employees:

- understand the benefits of their offer

- can recognise customers requiring that offer

- are empowered to make the offer.

Building high value, loyal relationships is the crux of the marketing conundrum and is the most powerful driver for success. Rewarding employees who have taken the trouble to understand and recognise such relationships is essential. Similarly asking customers for their feedback to check that the field of play is not shifting is also important.

Perhaps not to be recommended, but illustrating the need to keep fully in touch with customers and their tolerance for change, the CEO of Amazon.com has said:

> 'I encourage everyone who works at Amazon to wake up terrified every morning. They should be afraid of our customers. Those are the folks who send us money. That is why our strategy is to say; heads down, focus on the customer, because the customer needs change at a slower rate.'

Communicating values

Understanding what motivates your customers and similarly what motivates your staff is essential. If you know this information about your customers and staff, do you know whether it is shared with everyone at all levels of the organisation? The value of knowing your customers and the influences on your customers is illustrated in the following case example.

> Take BP, a company that has prided itself for many years on shareholder values and the quality of its product. A sea change has taken place in the last year or so that has led the company to start to promote itself on the basis of its environmental credentials. Its values are starting to shift with public perceptions about global warming and environmental change. The company has always taken its environmental liabilities very seriously, the change has been in the way it wants to tell the community first and foremost that this is what it values. They are confident to do this in the knowledge that shareholders will now see this as a positive move, it is likely to enhance its reputation for quality and it will strike a positive chord with the general public.

Talking about climate change BP says on its website:

> As a global energy company, we believe we can play a major part in finding and implementing solutions to one of the greatest challenges of this century.

Talking about business ethics BP reiterates its commitment to people and responsibility:

We believe running an ethical business is the right thing to do. Our new code of conduct, our ethics and compliance certification process, and OpenTalk, our employee concerns programme, can all help us achieve this.

Source: www.bp.com

Internally a company can make a very positive impact on results by changing the attitudes and beliefs of employees about the product or service offer. Employees are looking for elements of their organisation that they can be proud to talk about, that they can promote and feel good about as a team. They are looking for values that they can espouse.

Take McDonalds, a company racked by criticism of its high fat, high sugar food. The marketing and product development of the company now focuses on food, nutrition and fitness. They recognised that their key customers were fed up with defending themselves for using the convenience of a McDonalds store. Price was not a significant factor any more, instead people wanted to feel good about their decision to go to McDonalds. By promoting, messages about combining the food with exercise, and reducing portion size McDonalds was making a seismic shift in their own values to respond to the changing values of their customers. The result has been a happier workforce able to feel better about their role in providing food quickly and conveniently.

McDonald's wants to lead our industry on the well-being issues so many of our customers care about. Helping people achieve the right balance between the energy they consume as food and the energy they burn in physical activity calls for involvement and collaboration by many sectors. We aim to play an important role.

'We have a responsibility to lead. But more important, we can and will make a difference.'

Source: Jim Skinner, Vice Chairman & CEO
www.mcdonalds.com

Both of these examples show how external influences have led to a turnaround in the way organisations talk to customers and their staff. A changing world environment and much faster and effective communications means that criticisms can be broadcast far more quickly. Companies must respond to the needs of their customers more effectively before employees and customers become demotivated.

Activity 6
Creating values

Objectives

This activity will help you to:

◆ understand the values that are important to your customers

◆ recognise how customer values transform into the services and products you provide.

Remember the initial propositions ...

> Teams that share values are likely to work together better than those who do not.
>
> Organisations that share values with their customers and express those values are more likely to have a meaningful relationship.

How well to they apply in your organisation?

Task

1 Identify strategies used by you or your colleagues in your organisation to empower individuals and increase work satisfaction. Think back to your responses to the last task and what works well.

2 What specific means do you use to share values and discuss the values of your customers?

3 Think about ways your organisation shares its values with customers. Make notes on the areas you share values with your customers and how you communicate your values.

4 What evidence can you find that this contributes to more satisfied customers? This is a difficult one, it may be found in general 'feel good', feedback from employees or customers, increased use of websites for instance.

Feedback

This activity will help you to recognise the value of feeling good about what you sell and the way this impacts on customer behaviour. It may come as a surprise the types of message the company or organisation expresses, or it may feel entirely natural. It is useful to think about the impact you can have in this area and what changes you could make. It is worth looking on your organisation's website to review the messages the organisation is sending out. Alternatively you could ask a range of people you know (external to the organisation) about their perceptions of your organisation. Don't forget to consider how you communicate with internal customers and the values that you share with them.

Managing the relationship

Key account management and customer relationship management are two dominating themes in market orientation. The aim here is to explore what each can offer a manager in their toolkit to support cultural and business growth. More detailed knowledge of the concepts and functions of each can readily be found in marketing literature. The actual operation of systems and technologies is not likely to be a feature of most manager's roles, but a knowledge of the benefits is critical.

Key account management is a business process with three main elements that allow an organisation to explore and capitalise on their valued customers. The three elements are:

◆ an approach to customer segmentation

◆ the basis for customer retention

◆ a strategy for growth and development.

Customer relationship management is a technological system to support the management of relationships with customers or a business philosophy that supports the development of long-term, sustainable and valued relationships with customers. This concept moves on from the transactional sales model adopted for short-term gain.

We start with a review of the elements of key account management.

Customer segmentation

The starting point for key account management is to understand the values espoused by the target market at a minute level. Whether key accounts are individuals or corporate buyers, the foundation for customer focus is to know their characteristics.

Typically, it should be possible to answer the following questions about your key accounts.

Do you know:

♦ what elements of your service your customers value?

♦ what elements of your products/ service cause most difficulty for your customers?

♦ how much each of your key customers spends with your company?

♦ what proportion this is of their total spends for this product or service?

♦ how financially healthy are your key customers?

♦ what are their strategic plans?

♦ what processes your customers use to purchase, sell, manufacture or use products or services?

♦ what else your customers buy?

♦ what they buy from your competitors?

♦ how they rate your services/products?

♦ how much it costs to look after key accounts?

♦ the profitability of key accounts?

♦ how much it costs and what period it takes to replace a major new account?

The answers to these questions will provide the information required to target marketing and promotional efforts. They will also help you periodically to measure and monitor customer satisfaction.

Key account management generally allows an organisation to focus marketing communications more accurately. An example will illustrate how apparently focused marketing communications can go wrong when the organisation does not understand the values of the customer.

> A charity sends a specially printed, high gloss brochure to selected high value donators. The brochure is designed as a 'thank you' note depicting how their donation has been spent.
>
> The result: a set of disgruntled donators, furious about the apparent wasted cost associated with the brochure.

In this instance, the charity has not foreseen the reaction that the brochure is wasteful. It has not understood the values of their highest value 'customers'. It has not understood the elements of their service that their customers value.

Customer retention – supplier and customer relationships

The principles of key account management are based on meeting the needs of special customers more precisely. Recognising the value of key accounts and identifying the high costs associated with replacing key accounts will help to direct efforts towards retaining customers for longer and with a higher value.

Customer retention is achieved from the seller's point of view through the development of loyalty and customer satisfaction. It will involve tailored strategies for constructing and developing individual and corporate relationships.

Practical ways of retaining customers include loyalty cards, financial benefits, membership privileges and preferential treatment in terms of access to services or special offers. Many organisations email promotions and information, which serves to keep their brand at the top of a purchasers mind. It is easy to over reach with this kind of promotion, handled sensitively customers may see it as an important source of information.

Structural ties are another way to retain customers. The intention is to provide a range of services associated with the purchase that mean it would be more difficult for a customer to move to a competitor. Facilitating payment arrangements, legal agreements, use of protected patents and intellectual property are some examples. Offering groups of products which make the offer relatively unique can create a structural tie that a customer may not be inclined to break.

Reinforcing the purchasing decision and getting customers to understand the value of the service or product they have brought may also discourage defection. Customers may well feel a 'buyers remorse' or cognitive dissonance having made a large capital purchase. They need to realise the benefits of the purchase or the relationship quickly with after-sales attention. Recognition in the wider community of the good purchase decision is also a powerful force in overcoming cognitive dissonance. So, whatever positive messages an organisation can get out into the community around the time of a large sale will be appreciated by the purchaser and contribute to a long term relationship.

Purchaser relationships

Purchasers are increasingly looking at the supply chain to develop mutually beneficial links with suppliers. A smooth transition of goods, services and electronic data creates structural ties between customers and purchasers it also creates a lot of good will. The benefits of establishing a long term relationship with a supplier include, preferential services, trust, mutual promotions, benefiting from association with another brand, simplified payment and credit systems, simplified logistics and distribution.

There is a self-interest on both sides, but the customer relationship climate is developing to recognise that both customers and suppliers need to work at a relationship to get the best out of it.

Growing and developing customers

Understanding the potential for growing key accounts and retaining their custom is central to key account management. This demands, in some instances, some fairly complex customer and market analysis.

The dimensions that are commonly explored in customer analysis are described by Proctor (2000) as:

◆ who constitutes the market?

◆ what does the market buy?

◆ why does the market buy?

◆ who participates in the buying?

◆ how does the market buy?

◆ where does the market buy?

This analysis provides some detailed information about the types and range of consumer buying behaviour likely to be encountered. It may include habitual purchases, impulse buying, limited decision-making and complex buying decisions.

The process then needs to focus in on particular customers across the continuum from high value, high volume to lower value, lower volume customers. The kind of information required at this stage includes:

◆ actual current value of sales

◆ profitability of current sales

◆ cost of provision – services and distribution

- external factors such as overall market profitability, trends and developments, competitor developments and activities
- customer developments and capital growth areas
- predicted future demands
- predicted future demands can be assessed using a number of tools such as:
  - surveys of buyers' intentions
  - market research
  - sales force opinion
  - expert opinion
  - analysing past data.

Growth predictions need to take into account any diversifications in business or operations, new product developments, technology changes and demographics. There are so many variables that absolute accuracy should not be attempted. The principle aim is to grow and develop customers without expanding the organisation's cost base so significantly that the strategy becomes infeasible.

There are occasions when for the sake of profitability steps need to be taken to divest yourself of a customer or set of customers who do not fit the profitability/feasibility criteria. This allows an organisation to focus communications and marketing on those customers who deliver the best, and usually long term, returns.

Customer relationship management

The generally accepted purpose of Customer Relationship Management (CRM) is to enable organisations to manage their customers through the introduction of reliable systems, processes and procedures for interacting with those customers. CRM is normally envisioned as a set of technology tools. Typically there are three parts to the architecture of CRM:

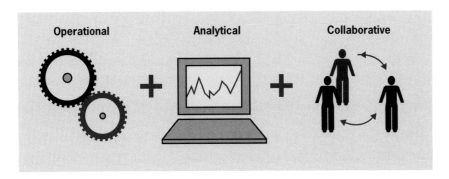

Figure 2.3 *CRM architecture*

A wider definition includes relationship marketing that brings in attitudinal and behavioural aspects of the relationship and forms part of the culture of the organisation. Relationship marketing focuses on improving feedback mechanisms with the customer and developing customer loyalty through knowledge and long-term contacts. Relationship marketing and CRM work well when operating together.

Partnerships

Partnerships, collaboration or strategic alliances allow organisations to concentrate on their areas of expertise whilst benefiting from the association with organisations with other expertise.

Partnership models

The Audit Commission have examined the nature and successes of partnership arrangements in the public sector and concluded:

> The common themes that emerge from our reviews are neatly exemplified by the recommendations provided to one metropolitan district council. The audit report wanted the council to have:
>
> ♦ a shared understanding of the roles, responsibilities and accountabilities of each partner;
>
> ♦ a shared ownership of strategy;
>
> ♦ better financial management, with clear procedures for determining the financial liabilities of each partner;
>
> ♦ performance management arrangements between individual organisations and the partnership;
>
> ♦ more structured and comprehensive reporting on performance and finance; and
>
> ♦ evidence of the value for money of the partnership arrangements.

Source: Audit Commission
www.audit-commission.gov.uk/reports

This provides a useful benchmark for all organisations looking for partnership rather than customer/supplier relationships. The crucial foundations of this relationship are a relatively mature market, product or service – which facilitates definition of service levels and trust between the partners. Suspicion of motives or veracity of the information provided by any partner by another is likely to lead to failure in the arrangement.

Proctor (2000) outlines the conditions that facilitate partnership:

Success is most likely where there is:

◆ Corporate compatibility – cultures and objectives mesh

◆ Compatibility of managerial philosophy and techniques

◆ Benefits for all partners

◆ Similarity between the companies that facilitates inter-firm communication

◆ Willingness to shut out others who are not part of the network

◆ Shared competitors

◆ Prior experience of successful collaboration

◆ Shared end-users

Partnerships operate on a spectrum of relationships from transactional selling to virtual integration of operations. The closer the partners are in terms of values, beliefs and behaviours the easier the integration will be. At the same time, organisations are keen to see new expertise within their partners to make the effort worthwhile. Much of the move to partnerships has been as a result of earlier outsourcing efforts. Outsourcing was seen as a one way rather than a two way process and partnerships are designed to redress this balance.

		Closeness of relationship
		Low — **Nature of the relationship**
Outsourcing	Arm's length	Purchase of goods and services from outside the company, possibly over the long-term
Partnership	Type I	Short-term focus, but co-ordinated activities between partner companies
	Type II	Longer-term focus with integration of activities between partner companies
	Type III	'Permanent' arrangement with partner companies highly integrated
Alliance	Joint venture	Shared ownership in an operation with a collaborator company
Ownership	Vertical integration	Full ownership of the activities or operations
		High

Figure 2.4 *Collaborative relationships*   Source: Piercy 2002 p509

Customers as partners

Customers benefit from partnership arrangements by:

♦ having a very clear line of communication with a partner

♦ understanding the processes, profits and mark ups used by the supplier

♦ defining and having their expectations clearly understood

♦ not having to contract for each part of a project or product purchase

♦ gaining understanding in a new area of expertise

♦ sharing experiences

♦ receiving clear reports on performance.

Suppliers as partners

Suppliers benefit from partnerships by:

♦ having clear and predictable sales of product or services

♦ being involved in strategic decision-making with partners

♦ not having to bid for every contract

♦ sharing experiences

♦ understanding the customers expectations clearly through regular contact

♦ a better understanding of the customer organisation and their end-users.

Whether deemed partnerships or not closer relationships with suppliers are becoming more common as organsations re-examine the supply chain for opportunities to create greater value for customers. The benefits can be considerable for organisations that are prepared to put in the effort to replace ad hoc transactional sales with co-operative and mutually beneficial alliances.

Activity 7
Relationship management and partnerships

Objectives

This activity will help you to:

◆ think about the way your organisations manages relationships with clients and suppliers

◆ understand how the relationship can be improved for mutual benefit.

Task

Use the following questions to prompt your thinking on key account, customer relationship and partnership management.

1 Does your organisation have a clear customer management process? What does it look like?

2 How might it change in the future to accommodate new ideas or changes in business strategies or as competition, technology and other environmental factors change?

3 Do senior managers understand the relationship between strengthening (or weakening) of customer management and overall organisational success (e.g. profit)?

4 Does your organisation have partnership agreements with suppliers and / or customers? What benefits and drawbacks can you identify?

5 Identify the key features of your partnership or customer relationship agreements with suppliers and / or customers.

Customer relationships	Always	Often	Sometimes	Never	Don't know
We have very clear lines of communication with partners and key customers	☐	☐	☐	☐	☐
Our customers understand the processes, profits and mark ups we use	☐	☐	☐	☐	☐
We make considerable efforts to understand and define their expectations clearly	☐	☐	☐	☐	☐
We have agreements in place that mean we do not have to contract for each part of a project or product purchase	☐	☐	☐	☐	☐
We seek to gain understanding in new areas of expertise and share our expertise with customers	☐	☐	☐	☐	☐
We seek to share experiences	☐	☐	☐	☐	☐
We aim to send and receive clear reports on performance	☐	☐	☐	☐	☐

Suppliers as partners	Always	Often	Sometimes	Never	Don't know
We have very clear lines of communication with partners and key suppliers	☐	☐	☐	☐	☐
We have clear and predictable sales of product or services as the basis for our agreements	☐	☐	☐	☐	☐
We involve suppliers in strategic decision-making	☐	☐	☐	☐	☐
We are involved in the strategic decision-making processes of our suppliers	☐	☐	☐	☐	☐
We do not have to put out every contract to bid or tender	☐	☐	☐	☐	☐
We seek to gain understanding in new areas of expertise and share our expertise with suppliers	☐	☐	☐	☐	☐
We seek to share experiences	☐	☐	☐	☐	☐
We understand each others expectations clearly through regular contact	☐	☐	☐	☐	☐
Our suppliers have a better understanding of our organisation and our end-users	☐	☐	☐	☐	☐

Feedback

These are challenging questions that you may like to discuss with other managers in your organisation. Your answers may not always be positive; that is the nature of organisations responding to change. Think about ways partnerships could improve relationships, logistics, supply, distribution and procurement arrangements.

◆ Recap

This theme explores internal and cultural changes required in an organisation to support a focus on customers leading to an environment that puts customers first.

Learn about the factors you can influence that make customers satisfied

◆ Your impact on your environment extends at least as far as the people you work with and your internal customers.

◆ The factors you can influence include, vision, attitudes, training in marketing and customers, understanding customers, hiring employees and employee rewards.

Evaluate your understanding of your own and your customers' values

◆ Companies are radically rethinking the way they 'promote' their images. They are looking at new ways of appealing to customers through values.

◆ The values that your organisation and your customers share are the most powerful ones.

Understand the importance of key account and customer relationship management

◆ Key account and customer relationship management are founded on improving your knowledge of your customers.

◆ Targeting and segmentation of customers will become more accurate and longer term relationships with customers are facilitated.

Assess relationships between customers and suppliers within partnerships

◆ Partnerships are set up to support long term relationships and offer benefits to both suppliers and customers.

◆ Partnerships demand more than just logistical fit. They are supported and made successful by shared cultural and behavioural values.

▶▶ **More @**

Payne, A. (1995) *Advances in Relationship Marketing*, **Kogan Page**
Professor Payne presents current thinking on the need to strengthen relationships with both internal and external customers to create customer value in the longer term.

Proctor, T. (2000) *Strategic Marketing An Introduction*, **Routledge**
This is an introductory text which examines the nature of marketing strategy and practices. It includes sections on the customer in the market place and targeting and positioning.

Piercy, N. F. (2002) *Market-Led Strategic Change: A Guide to Transforming the Process of Going to Market*, **Butterworth-Heinemann**
This book takes a fresh approach to the concept of marketing and seeks to debunk some of the myths. It has a central focus on customer value and creative strategic thinking in the context of realistic and practical examples. It includes sections on customer relationships and partnerships.

3 Positioning, branding and pricing

What makes them buy?

Key to the growth and development of most organisations is the positioning, pricing and branding strategy. As a manager it is useful to have a working knowledge of the fundamentals of this area, leading to an understanding of why customers, and in particular the decision-makers buy.

Some products and services are far more complex than others because of the perceived value or benefits associated with any given purchase. In certain cases, some products and services become elevated far beyond the basic core product, because they fulfil higher-level customer needs and therefore appeal to a particular segment of the market. A distinct product or service that combines a high price with a reputation for quality or prestige may occupy a unique position in the marketplace and may also be perceived to be superior to the other alternatives available. Conversely, some products and services that carry few additional attributes may still be popular with some segments of the market, provided the price is right.

In this theme you will:

◆ **Evaluate the need for positioning and branding or special identity to capture a position in the market**

◆ **Review pricing policies and pricing objectives**

◆ **Understand what factors affect pricing and positioning in the market**

◆ **Identify basic buying behaviours and the key decision-makers.**

Positioning

In 'Market-Driven Management' (2000), the author Jean-Jacques Lambin quotes the following definition by Ries and Trout (1981), since it passes the test of time and encompasses the key elements associated with positioning.

As suggested by the definition, positioning is all about developing a distinctive offering that is recognised and appreciated by the target market. Some products and services can be elevated, so that they are perceived as much more than a product, because of the nature of the marketing mix e.g. high price, high

> **Positioning is the act of designing and communicating the firm's offer so that it occupies a distinct and valued place in the target customers' mind.**
>
> **Lambin (2000)**

service levels and high quality Products positioned at the lower end of the market may not be valued by every market segment, although they may still be distinct and valued because they meet the needs of some customers i.e. they may be affordable.

Developing positioning strategies

In most cases, organisations do not have sole access to their target markets. To compete, suppliers therefore need to differentiate their product or service in some way, from the various other options available. This differentiation can take a tangible form e.g. based on the physical attributes of the product, or an intangible form e.g. based on perceptions and an understanding of customer psychology and buying motives.

In fact, competitive positioning requires the development of a total 'offering' that matches customer perceptions and fulfils a range of customer needs, including higher level needs, such as the need for 'status' or 'esteem'.

Common positioning strategies

The aim of any positioning strategy is to provide the customer with a basis for distinguishing the organisation from its competitors, so that it may be viewed as the preferred supplier to its target market segments. There are number of positioning options open to an organisation, depending on the particular circumstances involved.

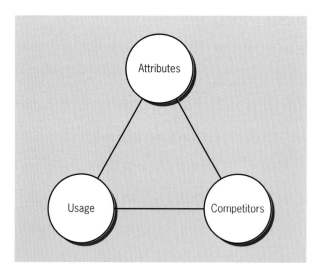

Figure 3.1 *Positioning strategies*

Positioning in relation to attributes

Product or service attributes include aspects such as product performance, product durability and the benefits desired by the consumer. A good example of positioning in relation to attributes involves the financial service and banking industry.

Because it is very difficult to differentiate 'financial products', financial service organisations often need reinforce other aspects such as security, reliability and stability.

Positioning in relation to usage

This involves positioning on the basis of use or consumption. Sometimes it is possible to identify particular use or lifestyle characteristics that appeal to certain users.

This means the product or service can be developed and promoted to meet the needs of the target market, such as in the case of low-cost telephone calls after 6 pm or over the weekend in the case of UK 'home users' of the Internet.

Positioning in relation to competitors

There are three basic approaches to this form of positioning.

Positioning directly against competitors
This could involve developing a product with comparable features to those of the main competitor, which is sold at a lower price than the competitive product.

Positioning away from competitors
Although a product or service might perform similarly to that of a competitor, in this case it will be positioned in such a way, as to promote the differences between itself and the competitive product.

Positioning in relation to a different product class
This involves the use of a slightly different type or 'class' of product or service, to compete with the more common alternatives that may exist. In some cases a less traditional or common option, can still meet the needs of the consumer.

Common positioning errors

Due to the complex nature of positioning, there are many potential problems associated with the development of a positioning strategy. From a strategic point of view, these problems can be grouped into four main areas.

Positioning Error	Possible Causes
Under positioning	The organisation either fails to successfully position, or does not even attempt to position or 'brand' the product.
Over positioning	Because of a very strong focus on one or a small number of attributes, consumers take a narrow view of the nature of product or the company concerned.
Confused positioning	This is usually the result of following too many options, or the diverse strategies of the competition, leaving the consumer confused about the image and values of the company.
Implausible positioning	This can occur when the claims made or the image created, does not appear to be possible or 'plausible' in the eyes of the consumer.

Table 3.1 *Common positioning errors*

What is a brand?

When a product occupies a distinct position in the marketplace it could be described as a brand.

According to McDonald (2002) a brand is about a relationship with the customer and in particular a relationship that is personified either by the company's name or by the brand name on the product itself. Here is what McDonald has to say about company and product brand names:

IBM, BMW and Shell are excellent examples of company brand names. Persil, Coca-Cola, Fosters Lager, Dulux Paint and Castrol GTX are excellent examples of product brand names.

McDonald (2002)

Developing and maintaining a brand (branding) is important to many suppliers, since individual brands are recognised by many customers. Branding a product or service allows a product or service to take on an additional 'personality'. In a sense a brand is rather like an individual, with its' own unique personality. A brand communicates with customers in various ways and can also be associated with certain values. If the values of the brand can be matched to the values and perceptions of a particular market segment, there is an opportunity to appeal to a particular market.

Branding can make it easier for a manufacturer to match a product or range of products to a market. However, it must be said that before a brand can be successfully established, there is usually a high cost involved. This is because a brand must be built and established over time, usually by undertaking extensive advertising and promotion.

Product and brand positioning

Brand strategies broadly divide into two main positions:

Brands which emphasise the corporate origins of a product or service – such as Heinz. Heinz makes a wide range of individual products all principally branded Heinz.

Bands that emphasise the differentiation of the product or service. Typically an organisation will promote individual sections of the range without alluding to the company name. This is common for organisations in the chemicals and cosmetics industries for instance.

There are a number of in-between positions where an organisation promotes the branding of a range or both the corporate and individual brands. Some organisations hide their brands completely from the end user and rely on endorsement from other brands, such as supermarket own brand labels, to sell the goods.

There are a number of advantages and disadvantages of branding strategies.

Brand strategy	Advantages	Disadvantages
Corporate brand	Strength of brand associated with all products in the range	New products have to fit with the brand values so more difficult to change direction
	Promotional costs are spread across the range	New product failures reflect on the brand
Multi brand	Allows differentiation of brands – there could be a low value and high value product available from the same company	Each brand needs to be promoted separately
		Market sectors need to contain enough potential to support more than one brand
	Existing brands are insulated from new product failure	
Range brand	The strength of the brand is conveyed to all the products in the range	New products have to fit with the range brand values so more difficult to change direction
	Promotional costs are spread across all the products in the range	New product failures reflect on the range brand

Table 3.2 *Advantages and disadvantages of branding strategies*

Source: Adapted from Brown and McDonald (1994)
in Dummond and Ensor (2005)

Activity 8
Positioning and branding

Objectives

This activity will help you to:

◆ evaluate how branding and positioning can contribute to the development of products or services in your organisation

◆ understand the impact of common positioning errors.

Task

1 Note down the key products of services produced by your organisation.

2 Make notes about these products under the following headings:

Positioning in relation to attributes

Positioning in relation to usage

Positioning in relation to competitors
◆ Positioning directly against competitors

◆ Positioning away from competitors

◆ Positioning in relation to a different product class

What risks would be associated with changing your brand?

Consider the brand – does it have a particular personality or identity?

Is the brand(s) part of a corporate, multi or range brand? And what are the advantages and disadvantages for your products of their branding?

Brand strategy	Advantages	Disadvantages

Feedback

This activity is designed to structure your thinking about positioning and branding in your organisation. It may be worth talking to someone in your marketing department or someone with branding expertise. Do you feel you know enough about the brand and how customers perceive your brand? Remember that a brand can be an asset and a liability depending on market conditions, performance and customer perceptions. It is an area of the business that needs to be constantly reviewed to check that it reflects the values you think you are selling.

Is the price right?

Pricing decisions are often the most difficult to make and price is not always the easiest element of the marketing mix to adjust. This is because many factors can affect the price of a product or service. Besides needing to consider the constantly changing micro and macro environmental factors, marketers must also take many other issues into consideration. Profitability and corporate image may be at risk if the wrong pricing decisions are made, so it is very important to understand the factors involved in pricing setting. Setting a price is therefore often much more complex than it first appears and is not just a financial decision.

Pricing approaches

Various approaches can be adopted when it comes to pricing a product or a service. Often the following approaches are used:

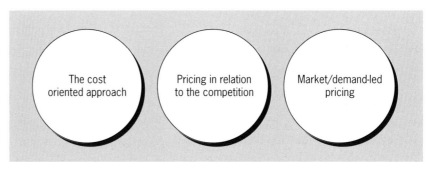

Figure 3.2 *Pricing approaches*

The cost oriented approach

The cost oriented or 'cost-plus' approach involves basing the final price on the cost of producing the product or service, plus an agreed profit margin. Although this approach is very simple to understand and in theory it might be a good way of establishing a desired profit margin, in practice this method can be a little dangerous. This is because the 'cost-plus' approach takes no account of the prices offered by the competition, or the price the market is willing to pay.

Pricing in relation to the competition

Pricing with consideration to the prices offered by the competition is a very a logical approach. The approach is based on the assumption that all competitors have similar cost structures and there is a little differentiation of the product or service involved. In practice no two firms have the same cost structure and it is not always easy to set a pricing structure, because of the other factors involved in positioning and branding.

Market/demand-led pricing

Market-led pricing is perhaps the best single method of setting an appropriate price, since it involves establishing the price that customers are prepared to pay in the market place. Using this approach may enable suppliers to maximize profit by charging a price significantly higher than they would have done by using a 'cost-plus' approach. On other hand, the price customers are prepared to pay may actually be below the cost of production, which would result in a loss unless other measures could be taken to reduce costs e.g. sourcing the product ready made from foreign markets to reduce direct costs.

In reality, each of the three methods indicated, should be considered when developing a pricing strategy. The final pricing decision can then be made with due regard to all the issues involved.

Pricing objectives

When establishing pricing objectives, it is important to understand and distinguish between pricing tactics and pricing strategy.

Pricing tactics and pricing strategy

Tactics relate to the short-term and strategy relates to the long-term.

Short-term pricing tactics such as the use of discounts, may be used in response to adjustments of the marketing mix by the competition, to reduce stock or to increase market share.

Long-term pricing strategies such as the adoption of a price 'skimming' policy, may be used to differentiate an organisation from the competition, or to support the positioning/branding policy of a 'high quality supplier'.

Increasing market share

Market penetration involves increasing market share, by selling existing products or services to more of the same target market.

A reduction in price would therefore seem to be a logical strategic option, when attempting to increase market share. Increasing promotional activity, or making it more effective is another way to gain market penetration. The combination of increased/more effective promotional activity and reduced prices might therefore also be a further (and more costly) option.

However, there are some dangers associated with the adoption of a price reduction strategy to gain market share. For example, price reductions could initiate a 'price war', as competitors will not be keen to lose their share of the market. There is also the possibility that price reductions could cheapen the brand image.

Increasing revenue or profits

Pricing policies also need to take the organisation's short-term and long-term revenue or profit objectives into consideration.

For example, in the short-term there may be a need to increase revenue for cash flow purposes. In this case, tactical pricing could provide the solution by moving stock more quickly through the distribution channel to generate the necessary cash flow.

In the long-term, bearing in mind that a company must satisfy its shareholders and its institutional investors, a desired level of profitability will need to be achieved. A long-term pricing strategy should therefore aim to achieve the required return on investment, while also maintaining the necessary degree of fit within the overall marketing mix.

Price penetration

Price penetration can be used both tactically and strategically. Tactically – this can mean setting low prices to gain market share. Strategically – this can mean setting low prices as part of a positioning approach. A note of caution must be exercised prior to embarking on any tactics or strategies that involve price reduction. Depending on the nature of the market and the competition price reductions could result in price wars, which of course can be extremely dangerous as far as the participants are concerned.

Price skimming

Price skimming can also be used both tactically and strategically. Tactically – this can mean setting high prices after launch because of little or no competition and the need to recover research and development costs. Strategically – this can mean setting high prices as part of a long-term positioning approach.

Factors that affect pricing

A wide range of factors can influence pricing decisions, which means price setting must not be undertaken in isolation.

When developing a pricing strategy, the following factors often need to be considered.

- ◆ Branding and how it relates to the price and values
- ◆ Competitors' prices and possible reactions to changes in price
- ◆ Corporate image and the effect of any changes in price
- ◆ Distribution channels and associated costs
- ◆ Political factors (taxes, foreign currency implications etc)
- ◆ Prevailing economic climate
- ◆ Product positioning and how it relates to price and value

- Price elasticity of the product or service concerned
- Recovery of research and development costs
- Return on investment targets
- Stage of the product life cycle.

Activity 9
An approach to pricing

Objectives

This activity will help you to:

- identify pricing strategies used in your organisation
- understand the influences on pricing in your organisation.

Task

1 Which of the following pricing strategies has your company used?
Make notes on whether they were short-lived or longer-term, and
how effective they were or are.

Pricing strategy	Duration	Effectiveness
Cost		
Competition		
Market led		
Strategic or tactical?		
Increasing market share		
Increasing revenue profit		
Price penetration		
Price skimming		

2 What are the main factors that influence pricing in your organisation?

Feedback

This is an essential part of the product offer and one that often influences all elements of the operation. Make sure that you understand the range of pricing strategies and whether they tend to work best as short or longer-term strategies. You may be able to find examples from people in your organisation of strategies associated with pricing that you were not aware of. Only by assembling as much information as possible can an appropriate pricing strategy be determined.

Who are the decision-makers?

Recognising decision-makers in the buying decision is a fundamental part of the customer relationship process. There are four basic buying situations:

◆ Complex new purchase – something new for which buyers may have limited expertise.

◆ Limited decision new purchase – something for which buyers need relatively little information.

◆ Straight rebuy – a routine purchase to the same specification.

◆ Modified rebuy – a more complicated purchase that is similar, but not the same as, a previous purchase.

Each may require a different decision-maker and various influences can be identified.

For instance, a straight rebuy may be purchased by a **user** of the product or service.

A **buyer** who has the authority to sign orders and make the purchase may handle any one of the buying situations. On occasions there may be a **decider** who makes the final buying decision – this could be the same as the buyer. There are also often **influencers** who affect the buying decision in different ways – i.e. through technical specifications, contacts, and previous experience.

On the other hand, there may also be **gatekeepers**. It is the role of the gatekeeper to ensure compliance with legal and internal purchasing policies.

Navigation through the decision-making process can be a complex process, but what influences do you need to look out for in the decision-maker or the set of people that makes the decision (decision-making unit). Proctor (2000) has identified 10 characteristics of buyers that may impact on the buying decision.

Buyer characteristics – Pyschological factors	
Motivations	Organisations need to know what motivates people to buy, what benefits they perceive. Given this information it may be possible to realize a competitive advantage. Motivations may be subconscious and difficult to understand or they may be related to needs where the most basic survival needs should be met first. An understanding of where a customer is now and their perceived and actual needs is a good starting point.
Learning	Most human behaviour is acquired as a result of learning from experience – this applies to the purchase of goods and services. Drives, stimuli, cues, responses and reinforcement underpin the learning process. So a drive becomes a motive when experience tells us we need something. The stimulus reminds us of that need. Cues are used to motivate people towards the stimulus. Responses from the customer are rewarded with reinforcement. Marketing and sales professionals use stimuli, cues and reinforcement to elicit drives and responses from potential buyers.
Beliefs and attitudes	People have beliefs and attitudes that affect their purchasing behaviour. Brands are related beliefs and attitudes and may be deeply ingrained. Marketing aims to set up positive attitudes and change negative beliefs if required.
Personality	Personality can often be categorised into types or groups. Personality may be defined in terms of life style, politics, culture etc. Marketers will look for relationships between products and personality groups and link them to images they can portray in marketing communications.
Life-style	Life-style groups can be identified and categorised to achieve an accurate portrayal of their key characteristics. Marketers use such groupings to target communications. For instance, people may be grouped according to their interests, their TV viewing habits, their habits in socialising or their family groupings.
Buyer characteristics – Social factors	
Roles and status symbols	People often buy products that relate to or reflect their role and status.
Family influence	Perhaps the strongest reference group which influences consumer behaviour is the family. As a consequence, marketers are interested in the roles and relative influence of the various members of the family in the purchasing decision.
Age and life-cycle	Different buying patterns are exhibited at every stage in the life-cycle.
Reference groups	Reference groups are made up of people who directly or indirectly influence a person's attitudes or behaviours. Marketers may make use of the language, terminology or media most prevalent in the reference group to target communications.
Social class	Members of a social class have similar values and attitudes in common. It tends to recognise job roles, pay, wealth, education and value orientation. Social class groupings tend to have distinct product and brand references.
Social background	People's social background is reflected in their culture, values, perceptions, preferences and behaviours. These may vary considerably across the world, and what may be deemed attractive in one part of the world may be of no consequence in another.

Table 3.3 *Buyer characteristics*   Source: Adapted from Proctor (2000) p151-3

Individual buyers make up organisational decision-making units. The difference in organisational buying is that they tend to be more proactive. Their primary concerns are delivery, price and service.

◆ Centralised purchasing has a number of implications for marketing of goods and services. There are more opportunities for the purchaser to strengthen the bargaining position and obtain lower prices by offering to buy a higher volume of services or products.

◆ There are more opportunities for the customer to develop a trusting relationship with individuals within a centralised purchasing function.

◆ Purchasing is more likely to be formalised in tenders.

◆ Structural ties can be formed to prevent defection of the customer.

However a decision is made, the consumers making the purchasing decision are individuals and there will be individuals who exert more influence at crucial stages of the decision than others.

Activity 10
Decision-makers

Objectives

This activity will help you to:

◆ identify ways in which you can influence attitudes amongst your team

◆ understand the importance of the internal relations in generating a customer focused approach.

Task

1 Consider one organisational customer or group of individual purchasers. Identify who are the:

    ◆ Buyers

    ◆ Influencers

    ◆ Deciders

    ◆ Gatekeepers

2 Choose a key one of these and complete an analysis of the buyer characteristics.

Buyer characteristics – Pyschological factors

Motivations

Learning

Beliefs and attitudes

Personality

Life-style

Buyer characteristics – Social factors

Roles and status symbols

Family influence

Age and life-cycle

Reference groups

Social class

Social background

Feedback

This analysis will support your understanding of your customers and their buying behaviours. You need to consider how typical this purchaser is and whether it can inform the way you work with a customer. Your customer could be an internal customer. The analysis will work in the same way.

Action list

Review the activities you have completed for this theme and write down any action points that you can use to support you and your team in creating or improving the market or customer focus in your organisation.

◆ Recap

Evaluate the need for branding or special identity to capture a position in the market

◆ Positioning is all about developing a distinctive offering that is recognised and appreciated by the target market.

◆ Branding a product or service allows a product or service to take on an additional 'personality'.

Review pricing policies and pricing objectives

◆ Setting a price is not just a financial decision. Pricing needs to consider market and sectoral factors, internal economics and positioning in the market.

◆ Pricing objectives include:
  – Pricing tactics and pricing strategy
  – Increasing market share
  – Increasing revenue or profits
  – Price penetration
  – Price skimming

Understand what factors affect pricing and positioning in the market

The factors that affect pricing and positioning in the market are:

◆ Branding and how it relates to the price and values

◆ Competitors' prices and possible reactions to changes in price

◆ Corporate image and the effect of any changes in price

◆ Distribution channels and associated costs

◆ Political factors (taxes, foreign currency implications etc)

◆ Prevailing economic climate

◆ Product positioning and how it relates to price and value

◆ Price elasticity of the product or service concerned

◆ Recovery of research and development costs

◆ Return on investment targets

◆ Stage of the product life cycle

Identify basic buying behaviours and the key decision-makers

◆ Key decision-makers can be individual or organisational purchasers. There may be people who influence the purchaser and people who impose restrictions on purchasing.

◆ Buying behaviours are affected by a range of organisational and social factors.

 **More @**

Drummond, G. and Ensor, J. (2005) *Introduction to Marketing Concepts*, **Elsevier Butterworth-Heinemann**
This text introduces the reader to basic marketing concepts. Chapters 7 and 11 are particularly relevant covering pricing and positioning, targeting and segmenting.

Kotler, P and Keller, K. (2005) (12th Edition) *Marketing Management*, **Prentice Hall**
Marketing Management is a resource designed primarily for future marketing managers. The twelfth edition incorporates new material brand management and includes strong sections on connecting with customers and communicating value.

Piercy, N. F. (2002) *Market-Led Strategic Change: A Guide to Transforming the Process of Going to Market*, **Butterworth-Heinemann**
Piercy covers positioning and market attractiveness in Chapter 8 and pricing in Chaper 12. This a useful text to support further learning on the theories that underpin marketing practice in organisations today.

4 **Customer challenge**

Improving customer service

What happens when customer service goes wrong and customers criticize, lose faith and leave? How do you communicate the value proposition to customers? Understanding the nature of your offer and the way you offer it should provide essential clues to addressing the customer challenge.

> **Coming together is a beginning. Keeping together is progress. Working together is success.**
> **Henry Ford**

Here we look at some of the elements of customer service that may need to be addressed to stay ahead of the game and improve customer satisfaction. This theme explores what product and service management means and how it can be improved.

Increasingly legal and ethical dimensions are an area of concern for many customer organisations. Find out how suppliers can turn them into a competitive advantage.

The final stage in the customer service process is to monitor customer satisfaction and after-sales service.

In this theme you will:

◆ Learn about customer satisfaction and what happens when it goes wrong

◆ Examine how the marketing offer can be improved through products and services

◆ Understand how legal and ethical issues can be turned to competitive advantage

◆ Monitor customer value and examine after sales service.

Products

> **Quality in a service or product is not what you put into it. It is what the client or customer gets out of it.**
> **Peter Drucker**

A product is often more complex than it first appears. Understanding the product and perhaps more importantly, the particular customer needs the product fulfils is crucial to marketing success.

We will look at:

◆ the concept of the total product

◆ product life cycle

◆ product portfolio models

◆ what can be done to improve the product?

What is the total product concept?

The total product concept is based on the principle that a product has more dimensions than simply it's obvious purpose or function. For example, a motor car is not simply a carriage that can convey its occupants from one destination to another. The motor car is a far more complex product, since in some cases it can fulfil a range of other customer needs including:

◆ Security

◆ Safety

◆ Status

Car manufacturers make an effort to understand the needs of their customers so that they can differentiate their product range to meet the needs of certain target markets. It is important for all manufacturers and suppliers to understand what particular features of a product interest the customer. Is also necessary to establish the key product benefits, which after all are likely to be the main reasons why customers buy a given product or in the event of disappointment fail to buy it.

Three levels of product

Kotler (1996) identifies three levels that make up the total product.

◆ The Core Product (the 'inner' basic product or the core benefits and what the customer is really buying i.e. a car or personal transport).

◆ The Actual Product (the additional features and associations that come with the product such as styling or quality i.e. a particular brand of vehicle).

◆ The Augmented Product (the supplier must offer a complete solution to their transport needs e.g. finance facilities and a warranty period on parts and labour).

The various layers that surround the core product add value to the basic product. The manufacturer or supplier may have identified these additional layers as important or key elements during the marketing research process. These additional product attributes may also create the opportunity for manufacturers and other suppliers of products and services to differentiate their particular offering from that of the competition.

One way of gaining a greater understanding of a product or service and also how to market it effectively, is to view it as a package of benefits. The success of each of the elements in the package needs to be reviewed constantly to see if they continue to match the requirements of customers.

The product life cycle

The product life cycle takes a product from the development of the initial concept to the ultimate withdrawal of the product from the marketplace.

Marketers are interested in product lifecycles because:

◆ the right products need to be supplied at the right time

◆ the market place is usually competitive and constantly changing

◆ the other elements of the marketing mix usually need to reflect the nature of the product and its' particular stage in the product lifecycle.

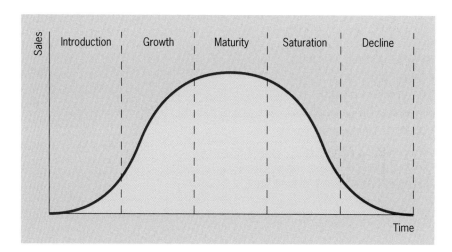

Figure 4.1 *The product life cycle*

At each stage of the lifecycle adjustments to the marketing mix (Promotion, Place, Price, Product) may be required. Some of the possible changes in emphasis involving the 'Promotional' or 'Communications' mix. The other elements of the marketing mix are also likely to need adjustment as the product (or service) moves through the stages of the lifecycle. For example, 'Price' and 'Place' are often likely to need some form of adjustment as the product maturity and as competition increases.

How can products be improved?

The importance of the total product cannot be over stressed. People do not habitually and loyally buy a product just because it is the best on the market. Instead perceptions are framed by a whole range of issues. The role of a manager in reviewing the product offering is to analyse and clearly state the benefits that the customer perceives – which could be anything from prompt delivery to the colour of the packaging. Unless you and the organisation are aware of these benefits, the buying patterns of customers are likely to remain a mystery.

Products and service offers are a balance between the skills and expertise you have to enable you to make the offer and the benefits of your offer as perceived by the customer. The improvement of product and service offers centres on the need to gain an accurate understanding of the changing needs of your customers as well as the provision of quality and value for money.

For instance, a customer may be attracted to your product based on price. Your organisation delivers the product on time and in good condition. Your customer comes to rely on the accuracy of your delivery and the condition of the goods. Price may not then be the principle concern of the customer. The changing nature of the relationship needs to be explored with the customer to ensure that you can continue to deliver the product they want on time.

This illustrates the complex nature of the product that is at the same time a tangible item and a set of relatively intangible services. It may well be the services that need to be adapted, rather than the product.

Services

Marketers of services are faced with an even greater challenge than marketers of tangible products. A product can be demonstrated to a potential customer who can also try it out, to see if the product meets the claims of the manufacturer or retailer. Services on the other hand cannot always easily be demonstrated and sometimes the only time a service can be experienced, is after the sale. Customers are therefore often likely to be more cautious when considering whether or not to sign up for a new service.

The product-service continuum

The term 'service' is rather general and can be interpreted in many different ways. For example, a service can be pure in the sense that it stands completely alone, or it can be provided in support of a physical product.

Although some pure services and some pure products do exist, in reality it is not always easy to distinguish a product from a service. In most cases, the offering provided by a supplier is actually made up of a combination of both a product and a service, as indicated in the diagram below.

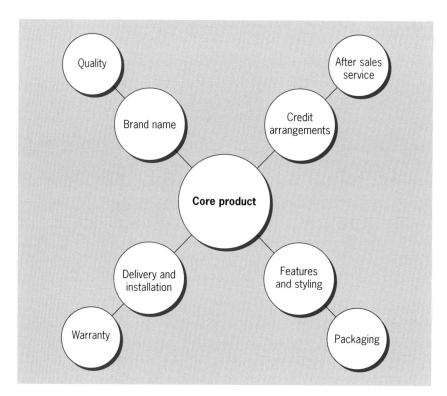

Figure 4.2 *The product-service offering*   Source: Kotler et al (1999)

In reality there is no firm dividing line between physical products and services, partly because everything has a service element, but mainly because, from the consumer's viewpoint, a product or a service may fulfil the same particular needs. For example, purchasing a new jacket may be as much of a spirit-raiser as going out on a night on the town.

Service characteristics

Because a service cannot usually be fully experienced prior to the purchase decision, consumers are likely to be far more cautious when making a service purchase decision. This of course often makes marketing a far more challenging activity for marketers of services e.g. holiday tour operators and financial services companies.

Although there are different service categories as indicated above, services share the following common characteristics:

Intangibility

Services, especially pure services do not have a physical dimension. If something cannot be seen and touched, it is difficult to demonstrate it's inherent quality. Marketing communications involving services therefore need to ensure that the features and benefits of the service are communicated effectively to the target audience. Building trust and a positive image as the supplier of services, is also an important part of service marketing.

Inseparability

Inseparability means that the production and consumption elements of a service cannot be separated. As the elements of production and consumption are linked, it is not really possible to fully demonstrate a service. The customer will only know for sure whether or not he or she is satisfied, after the service has been completed.

Variability

Variability (or 'heterogeneity' as it is sometimes known) can be associated with the delivery of services, because services are usually highly dependent on the performance of people. Since it is more difficult to achieve total consistency when people are involved in a delivery process, levels of service and quality standards may vary, even within the same organisation.

Perishability

In the case of a service, 'perishability' refers to the fact that many services are only available for a given time. Trains, buses, cruise ships and planes have to depart at a given time and if all the seats or cabins and not fully booked at the time of departure, revenue can be lost. The perishability aspect means that organisations must consider pricing carefully and develop pricing structures to encourage bookings while maximising profits.

Lack of ownership

Since a service is not possessed, it's existence and also it's benefits can therefore easily be forgotten by consumers. Suppliers of services also cannot repossess a service if the customer fails to pay for it after it has been consumed. Marketing communications associated with services therefore need to address a number of issues, such as promotion of the advantages of non-ownership in certain cases, or by constant reinforcement i.e. reminding customers of the existence of the service via appropriate and timely communications.

Defining service characteristics in this way can help us to understand the nature of the service provided. This in turn helps us to understand barriers to customer satisfaction. So if a customer is looking for consistency of service and finds variability, the service offer may need to be adapted to provide more consistency, or expectations may need to be addressed. Service characteristics are also useful in providing clarity about the service levels being provided, both for employees and customers.

How can services be improved?

In common with products, services can be improved by developing trust with customers and communicating with them sufficiently to understand what elements of the service they perceive to be of most value. The process for service improvement involves the following:

- Identifying the key service issues.
- Measuring customer preferences for the service.
- Benchmarking the service against competitors.

Once the service improvements likely to make a difference have been identified, there are a number of options for differentiating the service from competitors and raising its perceived value. These include:

- customisation to the exact requirements of the customer
- configuring the product or service to meet specific performance criteria
- benchmarking processes to raise the standard of operations and delivery
- defining service quality
- monitoring the process of delivery
- monitoring employee and customer satisfaction feedback.

These processes underpin the development and growth of products and services and the quality of delivery. Service quality and delivery are explored in more depth below.

Activity 11
Products and services

Objectives

This activity will help you to:

- apply product life cycle theories to your organisation's offer, highlighting any needs to review products or services
- review the process used to design and develop products and services including the need to test before entering the market.

Task

1 Identify how the product life cycle applies to your organisation's service or product offer.

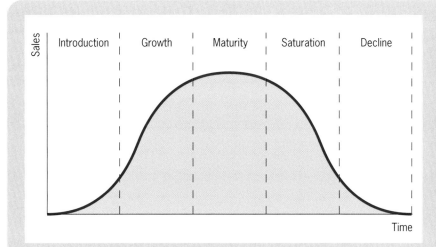

2   Create a diagram to illustrate how products and services are designed, developed, piloted and launched in your organisation. An example is given below for an Internet financial service.

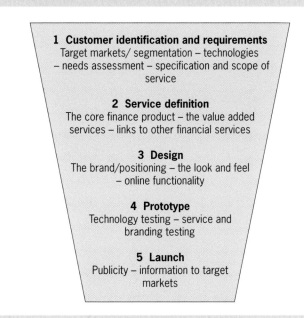

Feedback

The product life cycle illustrates the dynamic nature of the market and the predictions required of all managers in the organisation to keep ahead of the game. The essence of the life cycle is to forewarn of the need for changes and updates in product and service offerings. We can all think of occasions when a product or service has been continued for too long without the necessary injection of innovation.

Identifying the way products and services are updated and renewed in your organisation is important if you want to have a say in what the organisation provides. It is useful to be able to represent it pictorially. This may help you to explain it clearly to colleagues or your team.

Keeping the customer satisfied

Keeping the customer satisfied means understanding whether their expectations are being met and where possible striving to meet those expectations. Communication is at the heart of this process. Communication can of course take various forms and could be defined as the process of exchanging information or ideas, through the use of language, symbols, signs, behaviour, or through any technological means that result in an exchange process.

The 'Communications Channel' is the specific route we use to convey a message to the target audience. The route or channel may be traditional, such as via a 'face-to face' conversation, or it may involve the use of new technology, such as email.

Communication channels include:

♦ Advertising

♦ Brochures

♦ DVD

♦ Email

♦ Face to face contact

♦ Internet

♦ Instant messaging

♦ Letters

♦ Messaging forums

♦ Newsletters

♦ Telephone

♦ Text messaging

The medium used needs to match and access target customers precisely to be effective. More and more data is stored by organisations about customers, which supports very tightly focused communication techniques.

Communicating the value proposition and improving customer satisfaction

Customer satisfaction can be improved in a number of ways. The following are some of the key ways to communicate the value proposition of your organisation.

CRM

Customer Relationship Management is based on principles of effective data exchange, the purpose of which is to manage the total customer. By analysing trends and buying patterns, it should be possible to predict changes in behaviour more rapidly and to respond with new or adapted offers. It should also be possible to maintain consistent and updated data on customers to facilitate communications between the customer and a range of customer service employees. CRM can facilitate the process of one-to-one marketing – dialogue marketing. The employee has a full record of customer interactions on the screen.

Getting close to customers

Retention of customers has proven to be the most cost effective way of selling products and services. Achieving this and attracting new customers is all about getting close to them and understanding their motivations and their complaints.

A company that isn't there to hear the complaint of their customer won't learn the important lessons for improvement of their product or service.

> I won't complain. I just won't come back.
>
> **Brown & Williamson Tobacco ad**

Standards of service

Clarity of purpose for both employees and customers is paramount in the battle to balance perceptions and expectations. Employees need to know exactly what standards of service they are working to and customers need to know exactly what standards of service they can expect to receive.

A typical example illustrates this principle from the UK Inland Revenue:

Responding to post
We aim to respond fully within 15 working days. Our target is to achieve this in at least 80% of cases. Where we cannot do this, we will let you know the reason for the delay and tell you when you can expect a full reply.

Attending to callers
We aim to see everyone who calls at our Inland Revenue Enquiry Centres without an appointment within 15 minutes. Our target is 95% of callers. In addition, if you have an appointment you should not have to wait more than 10 minutes.

Source: www.hmrc.gov.uk/servicestandards/standards.htm

Centrica publicise their standards for customer relations:

Customer relations

We are committed to ensuring all our customers receive the best possible service. However, we recognise that on occasions, some of our customers experience problems.

We recognise that complaints are a valuable form of feedback on our service delivery. We therefore use this direct feedback to identify the root causes of complaints and ensure that improvements are made to our processes for the long term.

Through regular dialogue with our customers, we understand what the important factors are when dealing with organisations.

These are:

◆ we will listen to, understand and care about why you are dissatisfied

◆ we will endeavour to resolve your problem at the first point of contact that you make with us

◆ we will take ownership of your complaint to ensure resolution

◆ we will offer fair solutions quickly.

It is our aim to continually improve our service delivery to develop long-term and loyal relationships with all customers in all our businesses.

Source: www.centrica.co.uk/index.asp?pageid=33

In making its standards public Centrica is demonstrating a commitment to the public they serve and qualifying the way they will deal with complaints. This sends out a powerful message of commitment and clarity in their dealings with customers. This is what they will be measured on.

Training

An essential part of any customer service practice is employees' knowledge of what they can do to satisfy and rectify customer problems. Training is a fundamental tool to develop employee capabilities and understanding about what the customer is looking for and what they value. Employees need to know what resources are available to them to help satisfy customers' requirements and at what point they need to let customers go. Training can help employees to identify and implement clear and effective processes to support customers and sort out their problems without the problems escalating. Finally training needs to help employees in all areas of the organisation recognise problems, monitor customer feedback and understand how they can contribute to the solution.

Employees need to be encouraged to ask questions, provide feedback on all aspects of customer interactions and maintain records. In doing so they need to identify their own learning needs. The ability to codify and pass on the information learned throughout the organisation will create a framework for knowledge management and corporate learning.

Reward structure

Rewards have been traditionally given for sales against targets and in the form of commission or bonuses. Sales measured purely against revenue and balanced against costs create a culture that emphasizes transactional or short-term sales and competition amongst sales staff. With the recognition of the value of long-term relationships, partnerships and repeat business has come detailed consideration of the most appropriate reward structures.

Customer and market orientation mean that it is no longer really appropriate to limit commission and bonuses to front line staff. Internal customer relationships need to be nurtured and recognised. Longer-term client relationships feature in the climate, as do integrated partner relationships. The environment is not a simple one of reward for sales made, it is a much more complex network of interpersonal skills and clarity of purpose.

As such rewards are changing and recognition may be in the form of changes of role, training as a benefit, equipment, flexible working arrangements, cultural changes that praise, value and respect people, communications that recognise achievement. An example from Rhone Poulenc illustrates how a reward system based on sales achievement was ultimately counter-productive to the growth and development of individuals.

'People were almost totally focused on what their performance meant in terms of money. This hindered healthy, productive discussions on performance issues. In the new system, no one will be judged with a performance label. They will be given feedback geared toward development and improvement.'

Source: www.performance-appraisals.org/cgi-bin/links

Key Point: Feedback and appropriate performance appraisal can be a key tool in the reward and motivation process that benefits both the individual and the organisation.

Complaint analysis – dealing with complaints

Analysising and dealing with the complaints of customers may seem a very obvious technique for improving customer satisfaction. It is one however that is usually handled inconsistently and without sufficient attention. True collation and analysis of complaints tends to be inconsistently performed in many organisations. Ad hoc arrangements may exist which will deal with the complaints of the 'loudest' customers, but rarely are employees incentivised to encourage feedback and by default complaints from customers. CRM highlights this as an opportunity for dialogue with customers and as such should highlight the crucial contribution customer complaints can make to the development and adaptation of products and services.

Dealing with complaints is a difficult process but can be made easier for front line staff if they know that the information will be valued by the organisation. Given this context, employees are likely to be more receptive, less defensive and friendlier in their attempts to diffuse difficult situations. Where complaints are valued clear processes are likely to be in place to empower staff to take remedial action.

Partnership arrangements – structural ties

Structural ties within vertically integrated partner organisations are possibly one of the strongest ways to support improvements in customer satisfaction. In this situation, both companies are working towards the same goals, in the same environment. They will have empathy for each other's situations and find ways of working through difficult situations if they have been set up appropriately.

Publicising successes

The power of after sales reinforcements cannot be underestimated. Even a customer with a complaint is more likely to be understanding if they believe that they have essentially made the best purchase decision for them. Publicising relationships and successes that reinforce faith and trust in the supplier are an effective means of complaint management.

Reinforcement of buying decisions

Reinforcement of the buying decision can be effected in a number of ways. It will serve to prevent the customer from falling into buyer's remorse – a perception of having in some way been ripped off – it may also lead to customer recommendations. Both are very effective marketing devices for future sales from the same customer and from new customers.

Examples of reinforcements include:

◆ asking for customer satisfaction surveys to be completed

◆ asking for feedback

◆ listening to the customer about any concerns

◆ press coverage of the deal or other similar deals with satisfied customers

◆ keeping in touch through newsletters or emails

◆ benefits or perks associated with the purchase – including upgrades or fixes.

Message management

Message management is essentially part of customer relationship management. It is concerned with co-ordinating all communications with customers. This is vital in large organisations where there could be many customer contacts and many points of contact from the supplier. Co-ordination looks more professional and can save both customer and supplier time, effort and money.

Legal, ethical and environmental considerations

Customer satisfaction is no longer simply about the supply of an appropriate product or service in the right time, at the right place. Changes in the buying process now mean that organisations acting as both suppliers and customers need to highlight their green, ethical or legally compliant credentials. These are passed up the supply chain and represent a significant value added element for the end user. We look at this area in more detail below.

Legislation and ethics

Legislation and ethics in the business arena mean more than compliance with accepted norms, guidelines and regulations. Companies now see them as part of the marketing mix and are prepared to promote them heavily. But first let's have a look at the kind of legislation that can impact on the marketing process.

Acts of Parliament

Acts of Parliament in the UK cover such things as labeling of goods and advertising of foods, the provision of remedies that do not match the descriptions or claims made for them, 'sale' goods and prices, buying on credit, guarantees and conditions of sale. It is important for any organisation to be explicit and clear about claims made for goods and services and to get legal advice about all claims made.

Managers need to be aware of their customers' rights and how these rights limit what you are able to do for customers.

Copyright and IPR

These are areas of the law that are increasingly blurred by advances in Internet technologies and the sharing of information.

Nevertheless, they continue to be the framework for many organisations in a variety of sectors that rely on patents, copyrights and intellectual property not only for income, but also for differentiation from competitors.

Data protection

Many organisations, especially large companies in the financial services and leisure and tourism sectors now use the latest technology and systems to capture, store and analyse data. Often a considerable amount of emphasis and attention is given to the mining of the data, while perhaps the issues surrounding use of the data and the legal issues associated data protection are given less attention or are less well understood. It is therefore usually beneficial when the senior management of an organisation takes a keen interest in the way managers within the organisation use and manage data.

An example serves to illustrate just one element of the law associated with Internet use.

The UK Privacy and Electronic Communications Regulations (2003) law limits the use of 'cookie'. It states:

> 'a person shall not use an electronic communications network to store information, or to gain access to information stored, in the terminal equipment of a subscriber or user unless the following requirements are met'.

The requirements are:

> '(a) the user is provided with clear and comprehensive information about the purposes of the storage of, or access to, that information; and (b) is given the opportunity to refuse the storage of or access to that information.'

Equal opportunities

Discrimination and equal opportunities legislation have made an enormous impact on the way businesses operate and behave. This has developed to the extent that organisations are keen to publicise their commitment to equal opportunities and recognise diversity as a powerful force for competitive advantage.

Health and safety

Health and safety is of concern to us all. It impacts at every level in the community. This is reflected in the negative effects of any health and safety breach on marketing efforts. Most customers would prefer to be put to some slight discomfort for the sake of health and safety than question the credentials of a supplier.

There are a large number of regulations and codes. Some of these are set by the government, and some by other organisations (for example the Advertising Standards Association).The Chartered Institute of Marketing (CIM)make the point that:

> Just in the last year, 21 new Acts, regulations or amendments that directly affect marketers in their daily activities have been passed in the UK alone. In addition there are a further 10 Bills before Parliament in 2005-6 that will directly affect marketers if they are passed, including the Consumer Credit Bill, the Equality Bill, the Fraud Bill, the Occasional Sales Bill, the International Development (Anti-corruption Audit) and the London Olympics Bill.
>
> And as the global marketplace becomes smaller, and more business is conducted via the Internet, marketers have to have increased knowledge of laws in other countries too. Across the marketing community, who can honestly say that they are fully aware of the extent of the legislation that can affect their work, and that they regularly check to make sure their marketing activities don't flout any of the regulations that exist?

Source: CIM Insights Team www.wnim.com/archive

The message is that marketers and managers alike need to take notice of legal restrictions and take expert advice to ensure that they don't send out messages that fall foul of the law or waste valuable resources.

Compliance is a good thing

On a more positive note, the CIM is keen to emphasise how compliance with the law is seen by customers generally to be positive.

So the word is out there! Compliance to the increases in new legislation, which is all too often perceived as an extra and sometimes as an unnecessary burden upon business, needn't be seen as costly or resource draining. New legislation offers many opportunities to present your company as one that practices and preaches Corporate Social Responsibility, one that includes staff in much of the decision-making processes that help to drive a business forward.

Source: www.wnim.com/archive

BP have addressed the issue of compliance and green issues head on with a stated code of conduct:

The code of conduct covers five areas:

◆ health, security, safety and the environment – including basic health, safety and environmental expectations along with some fundamental rules

◆ employees – covering fair treatment and equal opportunity, providing guidance for dealing with cases of harassment or abuse and highlighting our support for the abolition of child labour

◆ business partners – providing detailed guidance on the giving and receiving of gifts and entertainment, conflicts of interest, competition, trade restrictions, money laundering and working with suppliers

◆ governments and communities – covering such areas as bribery, money laundering, dealing with governments and political activity

◆ company assets and financial integrity – containing guidance about the use of company property, proprietary information, intellectual property, insider trading and data and digital systems.

The perception among customers is likely to be that BP is taking its corporate social responsibility seriously and this is reassuring. What is more prime time TV advertising is being used to reinforce the message with the general public.

Our global advertising programme explains how we are acting on the challenges of climate change, energy security, new sources of energy and our ecological footprint.

Source: www.bp.com

Good reasons for environmental awareness

There are good reasons for promoting environmental and socially ethical credentials and these are linked to actual changes in production and delivery of goods and services. Organisations are recognising the limited supply of most natural resources and their role in preserving resources.

◆ Environmental marketing is perceived to be an opportunity that can be used to help achieve objectives.

◆ Organisations believe they have a moral obligation to be more socially responsible.

◆ Governments are forcing firms to become more responsible through regulation.

◆ Organisations change to environmental marketing activities in response to pressure from competitors' activities .

◆ Organisations have modified their behaviours in relation to waste disposal or reducing wastage in the production process principally to reduce costs. They are keen to publicise these waste reductions.

Activity 12
Techniques for keeping the customer satisfied

Objectives

This activity will help you to:

◆ identify a range of methods to help keep the customer satisfied

◆ consider the potential for legal compliance and ethical values in a marketing context.

Task

1 All of the following techniques can be used to help organisations keep customers satisfied. You may be able to think of more. From the list, indicate in the second column those that you currently use in your organisation. In the third column indicate any that could help you work more effectively with your customers.

Techniques, strategies or systems to keep customers satisfied	Used now	Potential for the future
CRM	☐	☐
Getting close to customers	☐	☐
Standards of service	☐	☐
Training	☐	☐
Reward structure	☐	☐
Complaint analysis – dealing with complaints	☐	☐
Partnership arrangements – structural ties	☐	☐
Publicising successes	☐	☐
Reinforcement of buying decisions	☐	☐
Message management	☐	☐
Legal, ethical and environmental considerations	☐	☐
◆ Environmental marketing is perceived to be an opportunity that can be used to help achieve objectives	☐	☐
◆ Organisations believe they have a moral obligation to be more socially responsible	☐	☐
◆ Governments are forcing firms to become more responsible through regulation	☐	☐
◆ Organisations change to environmental marketing activities in response to pressure from competitors' activities	☐	☐
◆ Organisations have modified their behaviours in relation to waste disposal or reducing wastage in the production process principally to reduce costs. They are keen to publicise these waste reductions.	☐	☐

2 What standards of service for customers exist in your organisation? How effectively are they met?

Feedback

Your responses will be individual to your organisation and you may very well have some techniques to keep customers satisfied beyond those listed. Talk to colleagues about any that you think might have potential for the future. Think about the particular issues that you face in terms of attracting, keeping and growing customers. These will have an impact on the types of strategy that you use.

When devising strategies to keep your customers satisfied, you need to know what you are trying to achieve. This can be defined in terms of the standards of service that you would expect to receive as a customer. Are these adequately defined in your organisation? Consider what you could do to make them clearer to your customers (internal or external) and to your team.

Monitoring and reinforcing customer satisfaction

Monitoring and reinforcing customer satisfaction involves:

◆ understanding the expectations of customers

◆ measuring customer satisfaction

◆ reinforcing the benefits of the relationship.

Understanding the expectations of customers

Proctor (2000) discusses the factors that influence expectations. Generally, customers measure their experiences against a benchmark of the service that they expect to receive. Expectations are comprised of what customers expect will occur and what they desire from an encounter. An encounter above these levels is likely to delight the customer and below these levels will make the customer dissatisfied. A number of factors influence expectations including:

◆ the personal needs of the customer

◆ alternative services or products considered

◆ specific promises made by service providers in a bid to win the business

◆ past experiences.

It is generally recognised that customer expectations rise with time. An effective sales process will surface all the issues associated with a customers expectations. This should help the process of meeting those expectations.

Measuring customer satisfaction

The SERVQUAL model has become the most popular measure of customer satisfaction levels over the past decades. The authors Parasuraman et al (1988) argue that in order to balance customer perceptions and expectations the supplier needs to:

◆ know exactly what customers expect

◆ set proper service quality standards

◆ support employees in delivering quality service

◆ never over-promise.

The SERVQUAL model measures service quality over five service quality dimensions:

> **Tangibles** – the appearance of the physical facilities and materials related to the service
>
> **Reliability** – the ability to perform the service accurately and dependably
>
> **Responsiveness** – the willingness to help customers and provide prompt service
>
> **Assurance** – the competence of the system and its security, credibility and courtesy
>
> **Empathy** – the ease of access, approachability and effort taken to understand customers' requirements
>
> These dimensions have broadly stood the test of time in terms of defining customer service quality. The aim is to test the key aspects of an organisation's skills, capabilities, resources and commitment to service. The SERVQUAL tool is designed with 22 questions to identify gaps in each of these areas, which can be used to address service quality.

Customer surveys

Customers need to supply feedback if service or product quality is to be improved. Customer surveys in a variety of forms are useful tools to support measurement of customer satisfaction.

Complaint and suggestion forms of one way of surveying customers, but these are most likely to be used by customers after a dissatisfying event. Some organisations take a pro-active stance and call customers after a purchase or service delivery to ask whether they are satisfied.

Customer satisfaction surveys involve identifying the factors important to the customers, assessing their relative importance and assessing performance against these factors. Amazon and eBay have built customer satisfaction ratings into the sale of marketplace goods. The ratings provided by customers are an integral part of the service delivered and provide reassurance to the customer of the reliability of external suppliers.

A formalised approach to the capture of feedback from customers or potential customers is marketing research.

Marketing research

Marketing research ultimately provides information to support marketing decision-making. Different types of marketing research provide marketers with a wide range of data that can be used to gain competitive advantage.

The research process

To be effective, marketing research should be appropriate, systematic and objective. The research process usually follows the sequence below:

◆ Identify the problem (specify the research aims and objectives).

◆ Determine the research method (e.g. 'secondary' or 'primary' research or both).

◆ Design the method of data collection (e.g. to be captured via observation or questionnaire etc).

◆ Decide on sample (sampling frame, selection process and sample size).

◆ Collect data (e.g. via researchers or existing sales force).

◆ Analyse and interpret data (possibly involving editing, coding and tabulation).

◆ Prepare the research report (the document submitted to management).

Some examples of research methods include the following:

◆ Undertaking surveys to obtain a wide range of customer feedback involving the use of 'face to face' questionnaires, postal questionnaires, telephone questionnaires and Internet-based questionnaires.

◆ Using different types of response forms or cards e.g. 'customer guarantee cards' to collect additional customer data, to enable detailed customer 'profiling'.

◆ Testing out various new ideas involving experimentation or observation e.g. testing customer reactions to packaging using special eye movement devices, or testing proposed new advertising ideas or promotional techniques.

◆ Working with focus groups made up of small numbers of consumers who may or may not represent the potential target market, but who provide useful qualitative feedback (usually relating to their views about a product, service, advertisement or even packaging).

What is the real value of customer research?

The real value of the research is to find out what your customers really think and in what directions they are heading so that you can provide new products or services or adapt existing ones to meet changing needs.

Due to the development and rapid adoption of new technologies, the speed at which the commercial world moves today makes it difficult for individual consumers or even some corporate customers to know what they actually want or need at any given time. If asked about their needs, some customers would be extremely hard pressed to provide a meaningful answer, because they are not always able to keep up with the rapid developments outside their own area of operation. Research needs to adapt to provide a model that informs about perceived needs, future needs and current criticisms of the product or services being offered.

Research cannot provide the answers, but it should provide clues as to current thinking from customers. It is a starting point that leads on to prototyping, piloting and testing new ideas in the market. In certain industries, some customers are now looking more and more to their suppliers for advice and also for inspiration and this can become a major factor when determining which is the best or most appropriate supplier. This also means that some suppliers must be far more pro-active than they have ever been in the past if they wish to remain competitive and take full advantage of the opportunity.

Reinforcing the benefits of the relationship

Communications with the customer do not stop at the sale. All organisations need to consider and plan the after sales service that they provide to customers. This will help to head off any complaints, promote feedback and keep the channel open for future sales.

After a major capital purchase in particular cognitive dissonance is likely to occur. This is sometimes known as 'buyers remorse'. It centres on the notion that the chosen option will have some unattractive features, while rejected options will have some attractive features. Frequently a decision-maker will seek information to reinforce or justify the purchasing decision and will filter information that is favourable to the decision. Lancaster and Reynolds 2005 identify the marketing implications.

> The major implication of dissonance theory is that for existing brands in the repeat purchase market the role of advertising is essentially defensive. It should seek to maintain the brand within the buyer's choice portfolio and be aimed at existing users of the brand who are aware of the brand and who have formed positive attitudes towards it... Repetitive reassurance advertising should therefore, reinforce the continuation of the buying habit in the face of competition.

Source: Lancaster p192

Customer relationship management (CRM) systems will also support the process of after sales service arrangements. Knowledge of the customers' buying patterns and habits will be invaluable. Supermarkets are increasingly making use of the information that we let them hold about our buying habits to help them target new products and discounts.

There are other factors associated with reinforcing the benefits of the relationship. As we saw earlier, customers are looking for integrity and may demand high ethical values, and environmental awareness. Customers are increasingly looking for longer-term relationships where they can demand transparency and open information from suppliers.

Internal marketing will support processes of reinforcement and add credibility to messages from the supplier. Employees basically want to be proud of the service and products they provide and will talk more effectively if they trust their employers.

Perhaps the worst scenario for any organisation is a product or service failure. Marketing planning needs to have in place clearly defined messages to communicate and mitigate the situation. Employees need to know how to respond, what actions they can take and that there is a process in place to help sort it out. Customers need to know that the supplier is listening and reacting appropriately. These are important after sales messages.

Activity 13
Customer satisfaction

Objectives

This activity will help you to:

◆ review your current service levels for customer complaints

◆ evaluate options to improve the offer

◆ examine ways to monitor and evaluate customer satisfaction.

Task

1 Outline one or two occasions where a customer has complained and how it was dealt with.

2 Describe three ways you could jointly work with a customer to resolve a difficult situation – this could be an internal or external customer.

3 What could have been done more generally to improve the situation?

☐ Product changes

☐ Service changes

☐ Legal issues

☐ Ethical issues

☐ Communications

☐ Monitoring of customer service levels

☐ After sales service

4 Write some brief notes on the processes and techniques used in your organisation to monitor and evaluate customer satisfaction.

Feedback

Monitoring and evaluating customer service relies on information and feedback from your customer. Do you have adequate systems in place to capture that information and if so does the organisation make the most of it to:

◆ show that you are listening to your customers?

◆ improve products or services?

◆ make changes to systems or processes?

Are staff encouraged to gather the information and if necessary rewarded for doing so?

Action list

Review the activities you have completed for this theme and write down any action points that you can use to support you and your team in creating or improving the market or customer focus in your organisation.

◆ Recap

Examine how the marketing offer can be improved through products and services

◆ Products and services need to be dynamic to operate in a changing environment. There are a number of factors that impact on the way products and services change through time. These include the product lifecycle, social and environmental changes, competition and customer expectations. Looking at the total product concept can be a useful way of keeping the product and service offer up to date.

Understand how legal and ethical issues can be turned to competitive advantage

◆ No longer are legal and ethical issues merely a matter of compliance. Customers satisfied by the overall quality of the offer may be looking at other factors in their buying decision. Factors that are important include the environment in which the product is grown or manufactured, the health and safety record of the organisation, environmental credentials, renewable sources and the potential for using recycled resources.

Monitor customer satisfaction and examine after sales service

◆ Customer satisfaction needs to be constantly evaluated. The keys to doing this are setting standards so that employees understand clearly what they are expected to do, and gathering and capturing feedback from customers. A company must show that they are not only listening, but making changes in the face of feedback.

▶▶ More @

Parasuraman, A., Zeithaml, V. A. and Berry, L. L. (1988), 'SERVQUAL: a multiple item scale for measuring consumer perceptions of service quality', *Journal of Retailing*, **64 (1): 12-40**
This is a classic text on measuring service quality providing key indicators and a means of interpretation.

Kotler, P. and Keller, K. L. (2005) (12th Edition) '*Marketing Management*', Prentice Hall
Marketing Management is a resource designed primarily for future marketing managers. The twelfth edition incorporates new material brand management and includes strong sections on connecting with customers and communicating value.

McDonald, M. and Wilson, H. (2002) '*The New Marketing*', Butterworth-Heinemann
The New Marketing presents a comprehensively revised blueprint for the marketing process affected by technological developments and the associated 'information revolution'. Built around the leading concept of a value exchange with customers, it provides essential advice on how to harness the latest technology and incorporate it effectively into marketing practice.

5   Competitive advantage

Changing for competitive advantage

What do you know and how do you find out more about your competitors? How can you turn that information into advantage? This theme examines competitor analysis and industry sector analysis giving you the local, national, international perspective.

The impact of technology has been wide-ranging and far-reaching. Here we look at some of the key advances that have had an impact on organisations.

Finally, change brings risks. Managers need to understand the feasibility and risks associated with changes in the organisation.

In this theme you will:

◆ **Review models and techniques to help you examine your industry sector and your competitors to support identification of competitive advantage**

◆ **Understand the impact of new technology on markets and customers**

◆ **Understand some of the risks associations with changes in an organisation.**

The leading edge

Organisations need to identify and react to changes in the macro environment to maintain a leading edge.

What is the macro environment?

The macro environment lies outside the confines of a building or an organisation. The macro environment is not unique to the particular organisation concerned, although it will affect different organisations in different ways.

Typically, the macro environment that surrounds any organisation consists of the following elements:

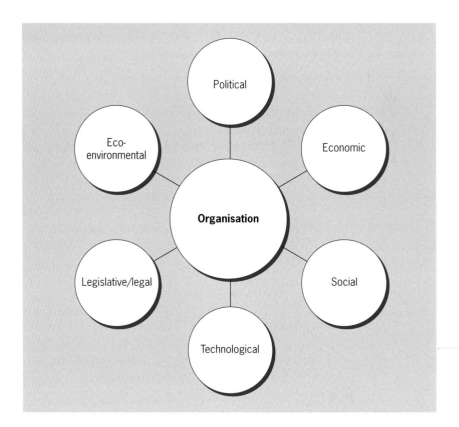

Figure 5.1 *The macro environment*

Since the various macro environmental factors will never remain constant, all organisations must pay careful attention to what is happening in the macro environment. Organisations that follow, or correctly anticipate macro environmental change will be better placed to take advantage of the opportunities that may exist, since some form of competitive advantage is likely to result if an organisation reacts appropriately to environmental change ahead the competition. As macro environmental changes can also present threats to organisations, businesses that are able to anticipate potential external threats will also be better placed to take appropriate action to address any internal weaknesses that could otherwise result in losses or even business failure. Dell Computers and Nokia are two examples of companies that have identified and then reacted appropriately to environmental change.

Perhaps this is an appropriate time to emphasise that all marketing and business planning tools need not necessarily be complicated or sophisticated. Sometimes, the most simple tools or techniques are the best to use. An example of a simple, but effective, analysis tool is based on the 'PESTLE' factors.

Marketing is really about matching the internal strengths and resources of an organisation, to the opportunities that exist in the external environment. The PESTLE analysis is an effective way of analysing the external environment and also the opportunities that might exist. An example of a PESTLE analysis is shown below, illustrating some of the opportunities that might exist for an Internet Website Design company operating in the UK.

The opportunities

As indicated above, the emphasis has been placed on identifying the opportunities in the following PESTLE analysis.

Political	Opportunities for the Web Design Company:
The UK government has set the agenda for digital communications and the take-up of broadband and digital media has been rapid.	This would indicate a potential increase in the demand for website design and in particular an increase in specific e-commerce products and services, such as the need for secure online shopping or 'shopping cart' facilities.
Economic	*Opportunities for the Web Design Company:*
In certain regions of the UK, businesses in key industrial sectors such as 'Leisure and Tourism', can apply for grants to assist with their own marketing activities. These grants can sometimes be used to help fund the design and development of an Internet website, to enable the tourism-related business to attract visitors, especially visitors from overseas.	Businesses in the 'Leisure and Tourism' sector can be targeted as grant funding will significantly reduce the final cost of a website. Opportunities may also exist to establish strategic alliances with associated businesses, such as 'language translation companies'. This is because many businesses will want to attract overseas visitors and 'foreign language' versions of their websites may be necessary.
Social	*Opportunities for the Web Design Company:*
The increase in Internet connections at home and at work means that individuals in the UK and global market are becoming much more familiar with the Internet and its various features and benefits.	Opportunities for the Web Design Company: When developing its advertising and communications, the design company can now place more emphasis on messages that aim to differentiate the company from the competition. There may also be opportunities to develop new associated products and services that take advantage of the Internet.
Technological	*Opportunities for the Web Design Company:*
Security is the biggest issue for most organisations and individuals surrounding web-based technologies.	Opportunities for the Web Design Company: There is an opportunity for the design company to provide secure site guarantees and advice or consultancy services. Many large and small businesses need advice on a range of issues, including the type of hardware and software they should acquire and how to ensure security.
Legislative/legal	*Opportunities for the Web Design Company:*
Legal constraints are becoming more apparent. Organisations and individuals need to ensure that the information they include is accurate and ethical. Intellectual property is a complicated area of law and one which is constantly being tested by website users and deliverers. An appropriate degree of care and attention is required.	Opportunities for the Web Design Company: This provides an opportunity for the web design company to provide consultancy services, advising clients on legal issues involved with Internet trading. The company may also look at the kinds of messages an organisation displays to establish their environmental, or ethical credentials.
Eco-environmental	*Opportunities for the Web Design Company:*
Environmental issues can cover a wide range of topics. For example, the reduction in use, or recycling of paper-based and other products is becoming a major issue at country level, at corporate level and on a personal level. Reduced use of paper-based products may be viewed as beneficial to the environment and actually save money.	Opportunities for the Web Design Company: Promoting the 'environmentally friendly' nature of websites compared to traditional print, may be a way of attracting attention to the company and may also appeal to certain market segments. Communications aimed at environmentally conscious customers and shareholders have proved lately to be a very positive and popular way to portray organisations on the web.

Table 5.1 *The macro environment applied to a web design company*

The threats

One of the problems associated with any of the various tools or acronyms used as a basis for analysing the macro environment (such as PESTLE or similar alternatives) is that managers tend to focus on only one dimension. For example, managers may place considerable emphasis on highlighting the various opportunities as indicated above, without giving full consideration to the various threats that may also may exist, or vice versa.

In the example above, it would therefore also be extremely important for managers to consider the various threats that could exist under any of the PESTLE headings. In a developing industry such as the one highlighted, there is likely to be considerable competition, and also a growing level of Government intervention. Certain questions will need to be asked and answered by management, such as 'Can our firm keep up with the rapid developments in technology fast enough?'.

The marketing information system

The Marketing Information System (MIS) as proposed by Kotler (1997) illustrates how an integrated system can be developed to provide decision-makers with the right information, in the right format, at the right time, in a cost-effective manner. The internal and external information should be analysed and presented appropriately to enable managers to plan, implement and then control all the various marketing activities.

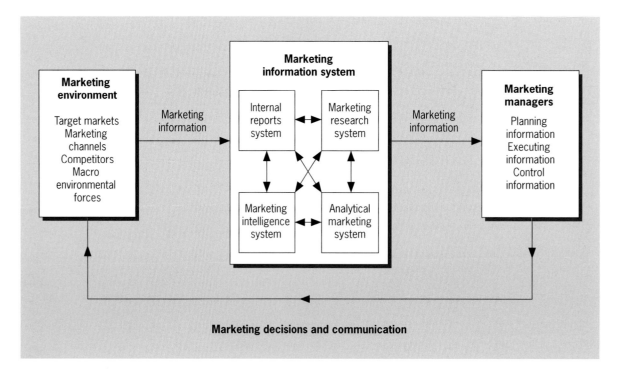

Figure 5.2 *The marketing information system*   Source: Kotler (1997)

A MIS can play an important role in providing information to assist with decision-making involving the following strategic options:

♦ New Product Development

♦ Market Development (entering new markets)

♦ Market Penetration (increasing market share perhaps by increasing advertising and promotion or by reducing price)

♦ Diversification (simultaneously moving into new products and new markets – the high risk option).

Quantitative Data

Quantitative data can be turned into information that might indicate the number and proportion of customer complaints received about a particular product or process, compared to the company or industry average.

Quantitative data involves numbers, or can be expressed in percentage terms to illustrate the number, or relative size of a market (or a series of events) e.g. our company received complaints from 5% of our customers, compared with the industry average of 8%.

Qualitative Data

Qualitative data can be turned into information that can be used to establish if a particular TV presenter is popular or not very popular with the target audience.

Qualitative data involves attitudes, feelings and beliefs and can provide an indication of the strength of opinion held by an audience or market e.g. 95% of the audience agree strongly that TV Presenter X should continue to broadcast the NEWS.

Marketing information myths

Piercy (2002) points out that with the advent of database marketing and the demand for more information often as an apparent aid to decision-making, there is a danger of creating information overload. This bombardment of data and information can result in executives becoming overwhelmed with facts, figures, reports and so on.

It could be said that some of the problems that arise in the area of marketing research and the management of marketing information, are caused or compounded because of the existence of a number of marketing information myths.

Managing Markets and Customers

The myths	The implications
We need more information	If anyone says they need more information, try asking them 'why?'.
We need marketing information faster	It is probably more important to focus what you are going to do with the information when you have it, rather than placing the emphasis on speed.
If we try hard enough, we can know everything	You can never have the most important information because it does not exist when you need it.
We know what marketing information we want	Surely, no-one still believes that managers know what information they want?
We know why we want the information	This may be so, although there is some evidence to suggest that much of the information collected has little relevance to decisions, since some is collected after the decision is made and some is ignored.
Well, we know what we don't need to know	Such arrogance is often the precursor to a fall, since managers are human and are therefore prone to lapses of complacency and occasionally fail to look outside the box. See the 'Reality Check' offered by Piercy (2002) to illustrate this point.
We measure what matters	There is evidence to indicate that contrary to expectations, we actually measure what is the easiest or cheapest to measure and this is not necessarily what matters.
We know what we know	Do we really, or in reality is our knowledge somewhat limited and do we just accept what we are told?
We know who decides what we know	Sounds reasonable, although this is not always the case since there is often some bias built into the system and there is ample evidence that once information systems are formalised people become far more 'careful' in the data they put in, and what they communicate.
Well, we know what it means	How often are companies wrong footed in the marketplace simply because they ignore important information for the reason that it is inconsistent with managers' past experience?

Table 5.2 *Myths of marketing information*   Source: Adapted from Piercy (2002)

Of course, many managers and organisations do manage their marketing information extremely effectively. However, the dangers of mismanaging the marketing research process or mishandling marketing information are very real and the myths of marketing research are a useful reminder of the dangers that exist, perhaps because of possible bias and complacency.

REALITY CHECK
Making assumptions and playing chicken
One of the companies, which shall remain nameless, that designs high-speed railway engines and carriages has a major concern with driver safety as speeds increase. How can you test to see if the windshield will resist being struck by outside objects when the train is going at 150 miles an hour? They contacted Boeing, who know about testing windshields on aircraft. They borrowed Boeing's testing apparatus, which was flown in from America. The machine was essentially a catapult. The instructions were to load the machine with a chicken and fire it at the train windshield to simulate collision with a bird at high-speed. This they did. The chicken went straight through the windshield, through the back of the driver's cab and stopped

only at the back of the carriage. The engineers were distraught. Boeing flew over experts to assist. They repeated the test with the same results. The man from Boeing smiled quietly, and suggested that they might get a better result if they repeated the test, but this time may be defrost the chicken...

Source: Piercy (2002)

Analysing competitive advantage

Competitive advantage is a process of identifying the competencies, or combined skills and knowledge, which distinguish and allow the organisation to compete.

Understanding the organisation's core strengths and weaknesses is an important precursor to any analysis of competitive advantage. A useful model for analysis is SWOT.

The SWOT analysis promotes strategic thinking about not only the strengths and weaknesses of an organisation, but also the internal and external opportunities and threats. This can most easily be achieved after the completion of the PESTLE analysis and looks at the micro, rather than the macro environment, in which the organisation operates.

The SWOT needs to consider factors such as branding, supply chain, market position, product advantages, new technology, perceivable changes in the market place and crucially feedback from customers. Identifying strengths should help to draw out the core competencies, skills and knowledge that are essential elements in the analysis of competitive advantage.

Porter (1990) identifies three generic strategies for identifying competitive advantage:

◆ Cost leadership

◆ Differentiation

◆ Focus

The way they are interrelated is illustrated in this diagram.

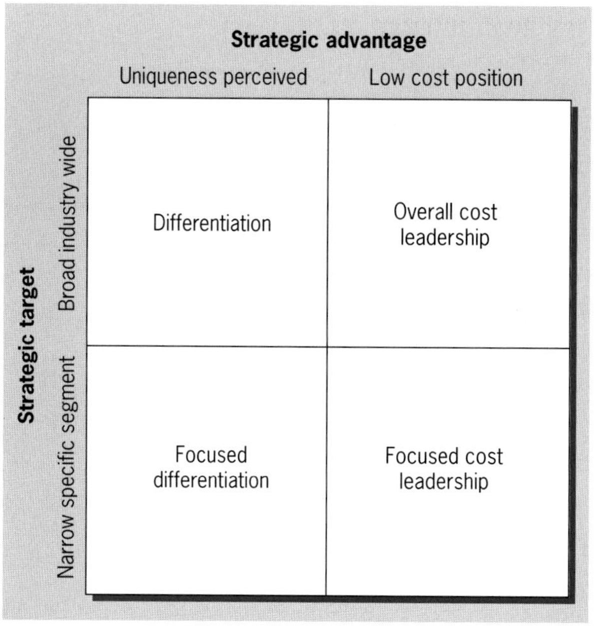

Figure 5.3 *Porter's strategies for competitive advantage*   Source: Porter (1990)

Cost leadership

Here the aim is to gain advantage over competitors by seeking to maintain a low cost structure and thereby reduce the cost to consumers. This is achieved through controlling overhead costs, economies of scale and cost minimisation in areas such as R&D, marketing, global sourcing of new materials and the application of new technology.

This is a difficult position to maintain and may attract attention from other larger and better-resourced companies who will seek to undermine your own offer. Cost leadership is usually associated with high volume sales and involves high initial investment costs. Occasionally this strategy will lead to damaging price wars.

Differentiation

Here the product or service offered differentiates it from others. The difference is based on providing value to the customer and should be perceived as being relatively unique in this configuration. It may be an opportunity to price the product or service at a high level. Common sources of differentiation include product performance, product perception and product augmentation. Product performance relies on factors such as quality, durability or flexibility and generally provides a tangible reason why customers prefer this product or service.

Product perception is more about the way a customer feels about the product or service. It relies on developing brand loyalty and is fuelled by advertising, PR and endorsements.

Product augmentation helps to differentiate one offer from another by the services or support that comes with it. AOL, for instance, are not just an Internet service provider. Their basic offer of Internet and email connection comes with a whole range of family and business friendly services that differentiate their offer.

The downsides of the differentiation offer are that if the offer is any good it will be copied and it also tends to be expensive and risky to set up.

Focus

A focused organisation tends to concentrate on a narrower range of business activities and thereby specialize. The specialism can be via geography or location, customer segmentation, or product line. This tends to lead to a targeted and satisfying type of organisation with very strong customer knowledge. However again competitors will try to copy good ideas and it is risky to have all an organisation's energies channeled in one or limited directions.

Porter's view was that an organisation should broadly pursue one of these strategies at a time. There may be scope for pursuing more than one and optimizing all available sources of competitive advantage, but in doing so, an organisation may risk the competencies for which they have become known – the benefit may be achieved at too high a cost. Another option is that an organisation tries to defend itself from replication by competitors and this can be achieved by using better equipment, by inventing new processes, by rewarding skills and by brand development. Alternatively, competitive advantage can be maintained by constantly seeking ways to update the offer.

A manager's ability or opportunity to impact on competitive advantage can be substantial and will depend on their knowledge of their customers, new technologies available and their understanding of the competitive market place. Most changes in an organisation are dynamic and organic rather than revolutionary. This is where managers have the greatest role to play in the sustainability and performance of the organisation.

Activity 14
Identifying competitive advantage

Objectives

This activity will help you to:

◆ analyse and understand your product and service offer within the context of the wider market

◆ review the competitive advantage of the product or service offer against Porter's model.

Task

1 Carry out a SWOT analysis of your organisation's product or service offer. Include the total product concept – the services that are used to support the principal offer.

Strengths

Weaknesses

Opportunities

Threats

Strategic advantage

	Uniqueness perceived	Low cost position
Broad industry wide	Differentiation	Overall cost leadership
Narrow specific segment	Focused differentiation	Focused cost leadership

Strategic target

2 Use Porter's grid illustrating the three generic strategies to outline your organisations competitive advantage. Which position does your organisation take? Make notes on the effectiveness of this approach and the potential for other approaches.

Feedback

These activities can sometimes be uncomfortable; they are asking you to examine some of the factors that underpin your product or service. Remember that changing for competitive advantage can involve small changes, where the impact is cumulative. There may be small tweaks that can be made to help your organisation work better with its customers.

The impact of technology

It is important to match the internal strengths of an organisation to the external opportunities that exist. At the same time, any internal weaknesses should be addressed and ideally eliminated, so that the organisation is not placed under threat by any external changes. One of the most dynamic elements in the external environment is the area of new technology. New technologies are continually being developed and these provide opportunities to some organisations and threats to others. All organisations therefore need to follow and ideally anticipate changes or developments in new technology to ensure that they continue to meet their customers' needs and create or maintain competitive advantage. Although some general technology and marketing-related issues will be addressed here, emphasis will be given to marketing and the Internet.

Technology – the opportunities and threats

New technologies are continually being introduced and many of these developments have a positive effect on customers. There can be an increase in customer satisfaction arising from greater convenience arising from the use of new technology e.g. 24 hour online banking. On the other hand, a technology-led approach can sometimes result in a reduction in customer satisfaction because of system failures, or a lack of personal contact.

Cringely (1996) described how Gordon Moore who later became Chairman of Intel, first proposed 'Moore's Law' in the 1950s. Perhaps surprisingly, 'Moores Law' still holds good today. An interpretation of Moores Law is that:

> Either computing power will double every 18 months, or the cost of computing power will be halved every 18 months.

The implications of this statement are that technology will continue to develop just as rapidly as it has done since the 1950s. Costs will also reduce significantly in relative terms making new technologies more accessible to suppliers and customers. These emerging technologies will therefore continue to provide new opportunities, such as enhanced communications and the opportunity to add value in terms of product (or service) development and delivery.

The opportunities

As computer technology continues to develop, so does the field of communications technology. Data, video, voice and music, are transmitted rapidly in a digital format. Communication and computer technologies are converging and this trend is set to continue. The trend towards convergence will be fuelled by an ever-increasing demand for information and entertainment wherever and whenever people want it. This demand will be met by independent suppliers and through mergers and strategic alliances such as between technology, publishing, media and Internet or network distribution companies.

Perhaps the most significant development is the move towards Internet-based communications involving high growth in e-commerce and messaging services. The increasing use of data and news transmission now takes place through mobile phone and hand held computers.

Consumers are making their demands and preferences known. It is becoming easier through databases and consumer tracking software to cost-effectively reach very small sections of society, even individuals. It is also possible to massively increase reach to individuals and organisations through Internet and email technologies.

E-commerce also opens up significant opportunities for organisations to capture and hold information about individuals and organisations. For the most part, if asked people have so far expressed little concern about the amount and detail of the information held about them on databases. Loyalty card customers register their details in return for vouchers or money off rewards and in return receive targeted emails promoting products that from the stores records would appear to be of interest.

E-commerce also makes buying and selling ordering transactions, on the whole, easier and more efficient. Organisations whose product offer is easily downloadable or purchasable digitally are seeing massive rises in consumer ordering via the Internet. Will there come a time when shops are a relatively scarce frontage for a huge Internet ordering system? A place where people go to try out and try on?

> It may not always be profitable at first for businesses to be online, but it is certainly going to be unprofitable *not* to be online.

Source: Esther Dyson

The threats

The range of new technologies is extensive and although the benefits to customers and suppliers can be considerable, there are some serious downsides associated with the development and use of some of these new technologies.

In theory the use of Customer Relationship Management (CRM), systems should improve communications and ought to help in the development and maintenance of the relationship between customer and supplier. CRM systems are based on sophisticated databases that allow data to be captured and then accessed by any authorised individual in an organisation. Often the customers' first point of contact is a telephone operator based in a call-centre, who can access customer records instantly, to deal with any queries or to take any new orders.

These systems may work very well, although in practice many customers do not find their contact with the organisation as satisfactory or satisfying as it ought to be. The customer data may well be available to the operator, but each time a customers calls, they may speak to a different operator and continuity and the personal touch is lost. Organisations are realizing the importance of personal contact and overly systematic operations are being phased out in favour of a real voice.

Every opportunity needs to be taken to communicate in a meaningful way with the customer, especially when there is a problem. There is no better way to communicate than in person either on the phone or face to face in this situation. However, for normal transactions people are beginning to prefer the speed and efficiency offered by technology.

The principle threats going forward, for most organisations using technology to conduct business, are infrastructure and security. Organisations are constantly responding to new requirements from customers, the market place and global communications.

> **Computers can figure out all kinds of problems, except the things in the world that just don't add up.**
> **James Magary**

Infrastructure needs to be robust and adequate to support the level and complexity of the traffic required. Computer fraud is similarly becoming more complex, more ingenious and constantly finding loopholes in software and systems. Organisations need to be constantly aware of threats and system changes that will support their own organisation.

The dangers arising from the failure of technology

There are many different technologies and systems used to communicate and add value in a modern business environment. Most systems probably do achieve many or all of their objectives, although when the technology fails it can spell disaster for the organisation.

The impact of technology or systems failure on the organisation and various stakeholders can be considerable, so it is important that new technologies are not taken for granted.

The Stakeholders	The possible implications involved
The Customer	Customer complaints and any associated costs may rise if technology-based systems fail. Customer confidence may be eroded and customer retention rates may fall. Customer loyalty may reduce as some customers will be more likely to consider competitive offerings and negative 'word of mouth' is likely to deter new customers, resulting in a loss of market share.
The Employees	If faced with an increased number of customer complaints, or if constantly bombarded with negative media reports concerning their employer, morale is likely to suffer and some employees are likely to become demotivated or stressed. Some systems may provide too much information and employees may suffer from 'information overload', or they may have to cope with an ever-increasing workload – which could in turn influence how they deal with customers.
Other Stakeholders	Because of adverse publicity, investors may lose confidence in the company and decide to sell their shares, which could have serious and more far-reaching implications. Depending on the nature of the failure or the nature of any publicity surrounding a failure in technology, suppliers may also lose confidence and question whether or not they should continue to supply the organisation.
The Organisation	Internally the company could be weakened by the effects of the system failure and also by the effects of a reduction in staff morale. The reputation of the company or the brand may suffer serious damage. Externally, competitors may well take advantage of the opportunity to increase market share by attracting customers through the use of various timely communications and perhaps by making adjustments to the other elements of the marketing mix.

Table 5.3 *The impact of technology or systems failure on stakeholders*

Damage limitation

Since the image of the organisation can suffer considerable damage as a result of any failures in technology, management needs to ensure that the damage is limited in the event of a failure. This means having a plan and the necessary skills and resources to react quickly and appropriately in the event of a problem.

Damage limitation may take the form of a speedy but well-organised and orchestrated public relations effort, involving the use of news releases and other techniques to take advantage of media interest, so that a positive and appropriate message is communicated to the various audiences involved. Since internal marketing will also be important, it will be necessary to co-ordinate internal communications to ensure that employees and any other key stakeholders such as shareholders are also given the appropriate information and assurances to maintain their confidence in the organisation.

The impact of the Internet

Although there are many new technologies that have an impact on marketing, the Internet is perhaps the most significant development to occur in recent years. The Internet is a network of computer networks and is not owned or operated by any organisation. However, it provides the opportunity for large and small organisations to promote and distribute their goods and services to a global market. Websites provide a 24-hour a day 7 day a week (24/7) opportunity for customers to view or buy. E-commerce facilities enable quick and secure payments for the convenience of both the supplier and the customer.

However, the Internet is far more than another advertising and distribution medium. The 'net' is also now being used for many business and marketing purposes including some of the following:

◆ Capturing data

◆ Improving communications

◆ Improving productivity

◆ Relationship marketing

◆ Research and information gathering

◆ Searching for possible suppliers

◆ Supporting remote working

◆ Supporting team working activities

◆ Competitive tendering

◆ The dissemination of information.

Many organisations are now using the Internet and more particularly the Web to create competitive advantage, by offering value-added services via their websites, such as free information and resources.

There are of course also various downsides to using the Internet, since it can still be slow and the right information can be difficult to find because of 'information overload'. Just like any other communications and distribution channel a website is not a total solution, since the nature of the product and the other elements of the marketing mix also need to be taken into consideration when developing a presence on the Internet.

> Web users ultimately want to get at data quickly and easily. They don't care as much about attractive sites and pretty design.

Source: Tim Berners-Lee original 'inventor' of the www

But does it work?

Piercy (2002) suggests that Internet-based trading is viable only to the extent that we can use it to improve the value we offer to customers.

Piercy also quotes Ghosh (1998) who suggests that the challenge to managers is to determine what opportunities and what threats the Internet creates. Ghosh argues that managers should focus systematically on what new things the Internet allows their particular organisation to do and identifies the following four types of opportunities:

◆ Establishing a direct link to customers (or suppliers and distributors) to complete transactions or exchange information more easily – adding to convenience for the customer, personalizing interactions with the customer and developing new services.

◆ The technology lets companies bypass others in the value chain e.g. distributors.

◆ The Internet may allow the development and delivery of new products and services to new customers.

◆ A company can use the Internet to become the dominant player in the electronic channel of a specific industry or segment.

Email marketing

> Research forecasts 48 billion email marketing messages will be sent, by 2007. Email marketing is currently a low marketing media channel. But the rapid growth from the current levels of email marketing (1.1billion in 2001) to the 2007 prediction could itself be a problem for suppliers and customers alike.

Source: www.wnim.com/archive

Email marketing depends initially on the email list either being self-generated or bought in. Effective campaigns generally treat the first email that goes out to a consumer as a way to generate your own data about the recipient. Recipients can be encouraged to respond with incentives relevant to the target market. If the recipient asks for the incentive then they must be the sort of person who is interested in the product. This data generation makes it a lot easier to target relevant customers, who have given permission to use their email address in the future. At this point, you can start a regular communication strategy to them to provide services, sell products or convince them you hold a valued place in their consciousness.

This ongoing communication strategy then gives a potentially endless number of opportunities to gather data and convert them into a customer for your organisation. It should also allow you to find out more about their perceptions of price and quality.

Mobile marketing

Technologies are converging at a rate we could never have predicted. Handset technology, mobile network links, message delivery, broadband data and user take up have all matured and reached a level where commercially viable and cost effective mobile marketing and data services can be launched. These services include text-messaging campaigns (quiz, votes, polls, contest entries), content downloads, instant voice response, community services, and mobile searches. You could be in a shop, try out a sofa and order it online from your web-enabled mobile phone. Your phone then may be able to update you with delivery details and provide messages to promote other items in the range.

Technology can support mobile marketing. The skills to effectively and engagingly target potential users providing a useful mix of information and promotion are nascent. Text messaging campaigns launched from the radio and TV have proved phenomenally popular. Highly targeted texts, for instance from estate agents, may prove useful, but the plethora of mis-timed and mis-firing text emails will probably only fuel skepticism in these early stages. Mobile devices are highly personal items and marketing leaders need to recognise the invasion of privacy that some messages mark.

In summary

Competitive advantage is about understanding where your organisation sits in the market, knowing as much information about the market and your competitors as possible and making best use of the technologies to support distribution of your product or service to customers. This needs to be balanced against risks, threats and feasibility of changes.

Activity 15
The impact of technology

Objectives

This activity will help you to:

◆ examine the role of technology in the production or marketing of your product and service offer.

◆ analyse the risks associated with changes in technology.

Task

1 Give three examples of ways that technology could be used to provide more effective customer interactions in your organisation. These could be small changes to systems or the introduction of new systems.

1

2

3

2 What are the risks posed by these changes?

Feedback

This is a key area for any organisation to gain competitive advantage. It is also an area that is constantly changing. The decision to take a technological route is made more difficult by changes in customer expectations and the costs associated with maintaining technological solutions. Your role as a manager is to explore the options and the medium term costs associated with them. You can do this by finding good sources of information and expertise about where your technology area is headed. Without this expertise, it is easy to make expensive mistakes.

Action list

Review the activities you have completed for this theme and write down any action points that you can use to support you and your team in creating or improving the market or customer focus in your organisation.

◆ Recap

Review models and techniques to help you examine your industry sector and your competitors to support identification of competitive advantage

- ◆ The models and techniques include:
  - – PESTLE analysis
  - – Marketing and information systems
  - – SWOT analysis
  - – Porter's strategic analysis

Understand the impact of new technology on markets and customers

- ◆ Technology cannot now be ignored either in terms of marketing, sales or distribution. Customer expectations are such that an Internet presence is virtually obligatory. This section looks at the opportunities and threats, the role of the Internet, email and mobile marketing.

Understand some of the risks associations with changes in an organisation

- ◆ The basic conundrum is to balance the requirement to change to keep up with customers and competitors, whilst maintaining the services and products that signify your organisation's expertise areas.

 **More @**

Cringely, R. X. (1996) *Accidental Empires*, **Penguin Books, pp. 41–144**
This work looks at the business of computing in the US, as computer science, as a business, and as a collection of extraordinary and eccentric characters.

Drummond, G. and Ensor, J. (2005) *Introduction to Marketing Concepts*, **Elsevier Butterworth-Heinemann**
This text introduces the reader to basic marketing concepts. Chapter 9 is particularly relevant covering analyzing competitors and competitive advantage. It also includes a number of e-marketing perspectives.

Piercy, N. F. (2002) *Market-Led Strategic Change: A Guide to Transforming the Process of Going to Market*, **Butterworth-Heinemann**
Piercy covers the e-volution of e-verything into e-business in chapter 4. This is a useful text to support further learning on the theories that underpin marketing practice in organisations today.

Porter, M. (2004) *Competitive Strategy: Techniques for Analysing Industries and Competitors*, **Free Press**
This is a classic text on competitive strategies and marketing covering competitor, market and structural analysis and strategic decision-making.

References

Bartram, P. (2002) 'The good the bad and the unprofitable', *Marketing Business, The Chartered Institute of Marketing*, July/August 2002, pp.22-24.

Brennan, R., Baines, P. and Garneau, P. (2003) *Contemporary Strategic Marketing*, Palgrave Macmillan.

Chartered Institute of Marketing www.cim.co.uk [accessed January 2006]

Davies, G. (2001) *Managing Markets*, FT Knowledge.

Drucker, P. F. (1999) *The practice of management*, Butterworth-Heinemann

Drummond, G. and Ensor, J. (2005) *Introduction to Marketing Concepts*, Elsevier Butterworth-Heinemann

Evans, P. B. and Wurster, T. S. (2000) *Blown to Bits*, Harvard Business School Press.

Ghosh, S. (1998) 'Making Business Sense of the Internet', *Harvard Business Review*, March/April.

Kotler, P. (1997) *Marketing Management: Analysis, Planning, Implementation, and Control*, Prentice Hall.

Kotler, P. and Keller, K. L. (2005) (12th Edition) *Marketing Management*, Prentice Hall.

Lambin, J-J. (2000) *Market-Driven Management*, MacMillan.

Magretta, J. (1998) 'The Power of Virtual Integration: An Interview with Dell Computer's Michael Dell', *Harvard Business Review*, March-April 1998.

McDonald, M. and Wilson, H. (2002) *The New Marketing*, Butterworth-Heinemann.

Murphy, D. (2000) 'Get ready for m-commerce', *Marketing Business*, The Chartered Institute of Marketing, March 2000, p.51.

Parasuraman, A., Zeithaml, V. A. and Berry, L. L. (1988), 'SERVQUAL: a multiple item scale for measuring consumer perceptions of service quality', *Journal of Retailing*, 64 (1): 12–40

Piercy, N. F. (2002) *Market-Led Strategic Change: A Guide to Transforming the Process of Going to Market*, Butterworth-Heinemann.

Porter, M. E. (1980) *Competitive Strategy: Techniques for Analysing Industries and Competitors*, Free Press.

Ries, A. and Trout, J. (1981) *Positioning: The Battle for your Mind*, New York, McGraw-Hill.

Schultz, D. E., Tannenbaum, S. and Lauterborn, R. F. (1993) *Integrated Marketing Communications*, NTC Business Books.

Smith, A. (1776) *The Wealth of Nations' Books IV-V*, Penguin

Smith, B. (2002) 'Give customers what they want!' *Marketing Business*, The Chartered Institute of Marketing, Sept 2002.

Srinivasan, S. S., Anderson, R. and Ponnavalu, K. (2002) 'Customer Loyalty in E-Commerce: An Exploration of its Antecedants and Consequences', *Journal of Retailing*, Vol.78, Number 1.

What's New In Marketing (WNIM), www.wnim.com